THE OUTHOUSE PAPERS

COUNTRY HUMOR & TRIVIA

BY
WAYNE ERBSEN

Native Ground Music

Order No. NGB- 956   ISBN: 1-883206-38-3

THANKS!

When I built my first outhouse (page 15) in 1999, I had a lot of help. Friends, neighbors and family came over and offered free advice, and some even held up the walls while I nailed. In the same way, I've had a lot of help constructing *The Outhouse Papers*. Thanks, gang! Barbara Swell, John & Lori Erbsen, Bonnie Neustein, Beverly Teeman, Janet Swell, Rita, Wes & Leann Erbsen, Lee & Nancy Swell, David Currier, Mclean Bissell, Doris Burgdorf, Connie Denault, Mary Brown & the Warren Wilson College Library, Loyal Jones, Bob Terrell, Joe Cline, Clark Buehling, Richard E. Hagford, Lynn Fox, Ron Huff & Don Page. Thanks to Steve Millard for cover art.

Library of Congress Control Number:
2002103192

Native Ground Music

109 Bell Road
Asheville, NC 28805-1521
(800) 752-2656
Email: banjo@nativeground.com
Web Site: www.nativeground.com

Dealer Inquiries Welcome!
Free Catalog

CONTENTS

CONTENTS

CONTENTS

CONTENTS

CONTENTS

CONTENTS

CONTENTS

9

FOREWARD TO THE BACK HOUSE

While I can't speak for you, many's the time I've visited the outhouse and found myself with nothing to read. If only I

had some morsel of wisdom, some tidbit of trivia, some crumb of humor to help pass the time during visits to the Johnny House, as some have called it.

So that you won't find yourself in this same predicament, I've put together this collection to help fill a vital need.

Open the book anywhere and let your eyes fall where they will. What you discover may make you laugh, chuckle or giggle but at the very least, will evoke a snort, cackle, grin, or grimace. If nothing else, you may find yourself emitting a sigh, a moan, or groan. But any way you slice it, this book is like the "board of education" applied to the "seat of learning." It will get your attention.

Let's make one thing perfectly clear from the get-go:

> ### YOU DON'T HAVE TO OWN AN OUTHOUSE TO ENJOY THIS BOOK!

In fact, you don't even have to "go." What's more, despite what the title of this book led you to believe, this is **NOT** a book of bathroom or scatological humor. Instead, it's a book of humor and trivia for both country people and city-slickers who enjoy a good laugh.

If you get a chuckle or two out of this book, we'd like to invite you to help us make Volume II even better. Please send us your favorite joke, saying, tall tale or bizarre fact. And who knows? Someday it may end up in an outhouse where it belongs!

Photo by Wayne Erbsen

The Old and the New

E ven before you read a book, you want to know if the author knows his stuff. Well my friends, I'm here to tell you that I know more than just a little about outhouses. In fact, in 1999, I built what several people have said was the finest out-house they had ever seen, or sat in. Let me explain.

In the fall of 1998, my wife Barbara and I decided that what we needed was a get-away cabin in the country. With a bit of good luck, we managed to purchase an historic log cabin that far exceeded our wildest dreams. Built around 1880, the cabin was located in an extremely remote section of the mountains of western North Carolina in an area known as Big Pine. Even before we closed the deal on purchas-ing the cabin, it was clear that I'd have to build an outhouse. "Going" in the woods soon lost its romance.

Being a city boy, I was less than handy with a hammer and a saw. But I seized the opportunity to roll up my sleeves and build a genuine structure. I was pawing the ground with anticipa-tion. The first thing I did was go to the library and wrap my eyes around a big stack of books on outhouses, both new and old. Some books went into the nostalgia of old outhouses, and a few even had plans for building a new

one. I was armed to the teeth and raring to go.

I knew for sure that an outhouse hole had to be dug about halfway to China. It was then that the light bulb went off in my brain. Just the day before, I had hired a backhoe man to put in a road up to our cabin. With his heavy equipment, surely he could dig a little outhouse hole for me.

Though I was patting myself on the back with both hands for having the backhoe man dig the outhouse hole, it turned out to be a mistake, a BIG ONE. To dig the hole, he used the big bucket on his backhoe. What this did was create a hole big enough to swallow a Volkswagon. As I was pondering how I was going to span this massive hole, the backhoe man shut off the engine and announced, "That's all she's gonna do." Mopping his brow, he said that when he got down to four feet he hit solid rock and that it would take dynamite to go any further. I looked grimly down into the gaping hole and told him nervously, "I can handle things from here."

Now that I was stuck with a Grand Canyon-size hole in the only place level enough to build an outhouse, I was bound and determined to build it there, come hell or high water. I climbed down in the hole and started digging. In a few minutes, I found the massive rock that had stopped the backhoe in its tracks. With a pick and shovel I did manage to break through the big rock and dig until I got down to around eight-feet-deep. But I had never worked so hard in my entire life! My wife Barbara shouted encouragement as my head sank lower and lower into the hole, as I tunneled my way to China.

Photo by Janet Swell

With the hole at last deep enough, I was ready to begin construction. But first I had to figure out how to span the gargantuan hole even

The author in the hole

before I started building the outhouse. So in addition to being a carpenter, I had to suddenly be a structural engineer to design a foundation that would bridge the gap over this enormous hole. As I was peering down into the hole, waiting for divine inspiration, my neighbor came over for an unannounced visit. He must have been sent in answer to my prayers, because unlike me, he is one of those handy people who can fix or build anything. With him as coach, we managed to span the hole with several locust trees. From there, things went relatively smoothly — at least for an inexperienced carpenter like myself.

After all the hammering and sawing was finished, I realized the job was far from done. Because the outhouse was perched on the edge of a precipice, anyone using the facility would likely step out the door and immediately plunge down the mountain. With careful attention to where you stepped, you might avoid such a fate during daylight. But what about when one of us makes a midnight journey to the outhouse? I cringed to think of one of my family members or friends step-ping off the edge and falling down the mountain.

Photo by Wayne Erbsen

The Finished Masterpiece

What was needed, I thought to myself, was a deck, and not just *any* deck. I soon built what must be America's only outhouse with a wrap-around deck. It was magnificent! As I sat back admiring my handiwork, I knew that the only thing it needed to be complete was a copy of **The Outhouse Papers!**

Abraham Lincoln was surprised when a man walked up to him and thrust a revolver in his face. "What seems to be the matter?" inquired Lincoln, with all the calmness he could muster. "I swore that if I ever came across an uglier man than myself I'd shoot him on the spot," replied the stranger. "Shoot me," Lincoln said, "for if I am an uglier man than you, I don't want to live."

Two weeks before the assassination of President Lincoln, John Wilkes Booth's brother, Edwin Booth, rescued Lincoln's son, Robert, when he fell between two railway cars at the Jersey City, New Jersey station.

Abraham Lincoln hated to be called "Abe." His wife called him "Mr. Lincoln" or "Father."

"If Lincoln were alive today, he'd roll over in his grave."
~Former President Gerald Ford

When Abraham Lincoln was running for President, a man named Valentine Tapley from Pike County, Missouri, swore that he would never shave again if Lincoln was elected. True to his word, Tapley went unshorn from November, 1860 until he died in 1910, when his beard was twelve feet, six inches long.

No photo exists of Abraham Lincoln smiling.

As President, Abraham Lincoln is said to have kept important papers inside his hat.

President Lincoln wore a size 14 shoe.

17

How do you tune a banjo? Tune first string up until it breaks and then tune the other strings to that.

Definition of perfect pitch: when you throw a banjo into a dumpster and it misses the rim and lands on an accordion.

What's the difference between a banjo and an onion? No one cries when you chop up a banjo.

How can you tell when a banjo player is sitting in a level spot?

The tobacco juice runs out of both sides of his mouth.

What do you call a banjo player without a girlfriend? Homeless.

How do you get two banjo players to play in perfect harmony? Shoot one.

What do you say to the banjo player in a three-piece suit? "Will the defendant please rise."

Jim Bollman Collection

"Doctor, Doctor, will I be able to play the banjo after the operation?" "Yes, of course." "That's great cuz I never could play one before...."

"A gentleman is someone who can play the banjo ... and doesn't." ~Mark Twain

BEAUTY SECRETS

I f you drop a spoon in the pickle jar while you are making them, you will be a sour old woman.

Eating burnt toast will give you curly hair and pink cheeks.

Eat a dozen onions before going to bed to become beautiful.

To be beautiful, wash your face in dew before sunrise on May Day.

If you want to be pretty, eat a chicken neck.

If your cornbread is rough, your future husband's face will be rough.

BEAUTY SECRETS

Comb Lore

 hen you drop a comb, put your foot on it and make a wish. It will come true.

Hair Superstition

If you pull a hair out of a girl's head, she will love you.

If you eat a hundred chicken gizzards, you will be pretty.

Eating cornfield peas will make you beautiful.

Eat carrots and you will be pretty.

Go behind a door and eat a chicken foot and you will become beautiful.

> *"Beauty never makes the kettle boil."*

Biscuits were first made for sailors to take with them on the high seas. To keep them from spoiling on their long journeys, they were cooked twice. The French words for twice cooked is "bis cuit."

If you take the last biscuit on the plate, you will have to kiss the cook.

If you drop a biscuit, you will marry a poor man.

"Burn the biscuits, and feed the devil."

If you take the next to last biscuit on a plate, you will have a handsome husband.

"Those biscuits are so big it only takes nine to make a dozen."

"She's got a biscuit in the oven." (She's pregnant.)

TWENTY-SEVEN MILLION BISCUITS

"I figure in all the years of marriage, she's made me 27,477,000 biscuits. Hmmmmm. They were good." Fred Wright, age 99, reflecting on 80 years of marriage.

Civil War Biscuits

Civil War soldiers cooked a dish called "Hell-Fire Stew." It consisted of adding stale biscuits and bacon grease to boiling water and cooking until soft. This delicacy was also known as "Burnside Stew," "Hish and Hash," "Son of Sea Dog," and "Skillygalee."

During the Civil War some Confederate soldiers used the ramrod from their rifles to bake their bread over an open fire.

Biscuit Sayings

Take two and butter 'em while they're hot.

Better the guests wait on the biscuits than the biscuits wait on the guests. ~*Maudie Smith*

Names for Biscuits

Sourdough bullets, hot rocks, gravy sponge, flour-tiles.

BOX SUPPERS

"**B**ack when I was of courting age, I could hardly wait until they auctioned off the box suppers. Although it was supposed to be top secret, we boys were desperate to find out which box our favorite girl had made. A fatal slip-up might mean we bid on and won a box made by some ugly girl, or worse, a married woman or spinster!"

"Of course, the girls often had ideas of their own. Although we wandered around in a state of semi-confusion most of the time, the girls' foremost goal was to further befuddle us by disguising their boxes."

"We thought we were being so slick by hiding in the bushes and spying on the girls as they arrived for the auction. But they outsmarted us again by trading boxes amongst themselves or by spreading false rumors about how their boxes were decorated."

"After the bidding started, sheer pandemonium usually broke loose when one of the boys was fooled into bidding on the wrong box. As he reluctantly escorted his "date" out the nearest door, box in hand, he was often showered by the hoots and howls of his closest friends."

hen his chickens started to get sick and quit laying, a farmer decided he needed to get help from the State Department of Agriculture. He picked the sickest-looking chicken, wrung its neck, and sent it off for evaluation. About a week later, he received a letter back in the mail from the Department of Agriculture. After analyzing the sick chicken it was found that it died of a sudden broken neck.

Farmer: *"Doctor, doctor, my brother thinks he is a chicken."*
Doctor: *"How long has he thought he was a chicken?"*
Farmer: *"Three years."*
Doctor: *"Why did you wait so long to bring him in."*
Farmer: *"We needed the eggs."*

Having a ten-toed chicken brings good luck. (Kentucky)

One farmer claimed he could do every job around the farm except lay eggs.

CHICKENS

Chicken Sayings

The hen that lays the biggest egg does the least cackling.

———◆———

Farmers' curse: Chicken one day, feathers the next.

———◆———

Roosters crow, hens deliver.

———◆———

Every cock fights best on his own dunghill.

———◆———

You can put a hen's egg in an eagle's nest, but you'll still get chickens.

———◆———

You can't hatch chickens from fried eggs.

———◆———

When an old hen cackles, she's either layin' or lyin.'

———◆———

"Eggs have no business dancing with stones." Haitian saying

———◆———

Girls who whistle and hens that crow make their way wherever they go.

———◆———

> *"A hen who has merely laid an egg cackles as if she had laid an asteroid."*
>
> *"Put all of your eggs in one basket. Then, watch that basket." ~Mark Twain*

Two city slickers bought a farm and decided to raise pigs. They loaded their sow in a wheelbarrow and took it to the farmer up the road who had a boar. They brought her back and waited, but didn't see any sign of the sow having piglets. Again, they loaded the sow in the wheelbarrow and brought her to the boar, but still no piglets. About the time they were ready to give up, they went outside and there was the sow, sitting patiently in the wheelbarrow.

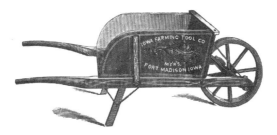

A city-slicker was motoring along a country road when he came to the scene of an accident. He could tell right off that a wagonload of manure had overturned. Then he saw a young country boy frantically shoveling manure everywhere but back in the wagon. The city man jumped out and asked the boy, "Say, aren't you a little young to be doing this kind of hard work all by yourself? Where is your father?" The country boy spoke up and said, "Why, Mister, he's under this pile of manure."

Boiled rye: Coffee
Butter: Strong grease
Coffee boiler: A laggard
Crumb: A louse
Death bells: Hardtack
Dog robber: Cook (N)
Embalmed beef: Canned beef
Fire 'n fall back: Toss your cookies
Fresh fish: A raw recruit
Goober grabber: Georgia soldier
Grab a root: To eat
Lincoln coffee: Real coffee (S)
Lincoln pie: Hardtack (N)
McClellan pie: Hardtack (N)

Old horse: Corned beef
Pickled mule: Salted meat
Pie eater: A rural man (N)
Pumpkin rind: Lieutenant (N)
Salt horse: Salted beef
Shadow soup: Thin chicken soup
Shucks: Confederate money
Sinker: Hardtack
Skillygalee: Grease-fried hardtack
Skirmish: To remove body lice
Stray: Stolen livestock (N)
Tennessee trots: Diarrhea
(N) Northern (S) Southern

A small boy was leading a mule past an army camp. To have a little fun, one of the soldiers called out, "Why are you holding your brother so tight, Sonny?" "So he won't join the army," replied the boy.

A soldier made the mistake of getting too close to the rear end of a mule. His companions caught him on the fly, placed him on a stretcher and headed for a makeshift hospital. On the way the soldier came to. He gazed at the sky overhead and felt the sway-ing motion of the stretcher. Feebly he lowered his hand over the side to find nothing but space. "My God," he groaned. "I haven't even hit the ground yet!"

Still bitter over Sherman's burning every building on the property he owns, one homeowner recently filed deed restrictions to prohibit "The Yankee race — those who were born above the Mason-Dixon line or who lived there for a year or more," from ever owning any part of his 1,688 acres. The restrictions also prohibit anyone named Sherman, or any Northerner whose names can be spelled from its letters, from setting foot on his property.

Stonewall Jackson in Heaven

When Stonewall Jackson died, St. Peter sent two angels for him. They searched the fields, the hospitals and even checked the whole army but could not find him. Returning empty-handed to Heaven, St. Peter told them, "Why, he has flanked you both. He's been here for six hours!"

The most popular song of the Confederacy, "Dixie," was written in 1859 by a Yankee from Ohio, Daniel D. Emmett. "Dixie" was also one of President Lincoln's favorite songs.

DAN.D.EMMETT.

"If I had known 'Dixie' would become so popular, I would have written it better."
~Daniel D. Emmett

During the Civil War, opium was used as a pain killer. By the war's end, 100,000 soldiers were known to be addicted.

The word "sideburns" came from the extraordinary set worn by Union General Ambrose E. Burnside.

Rather than join the Civil War, Grover Cleveland paid a substitute $150 to take his place.

At the first Battle of Bull Run in 1861, Barnard Elliott commented, "There is Jackson, standing like a stone wall." The nickname "Stonewall" Jackson stuck.

We have the Civil War to thank for our first income tax. In 1864 the Federal government enacted the income tax to finance the war. The Supreme Court ruled it unconstitutional in 1894, but in 1913 Congress passed the 16th amendment, making taxes as sure as death.

CIVIL WAR TRIVIA

Short on certain supplies during the war, the Federal and the Confederate governments traded essential items. The North needed cotton for uniforms, and the South need opium as a pain killer, so these items were traded.

The first battle of the Civil War was also the shortest. It only took the Confederates 1½ days to capture Fort Sumter. It was also the least bloody, with no casualties.

The largest painting in the world is *The Battle of Gettysburg.* When it was completed in 1883 by Paul Philippoteaux and sixteen assistants, it was 410 feet long and 70 feet high and weighed 11,792 pounds.

General Grant's most important secret agent was Elizabeth Van Lew, the daughter of a well-to-do Richmond, Virginia merchant. Known as "Crazy Bet," she easily passed secrets to Union commanders and even hid escaped Union soldiers in her mansion.

CIVIL WAR TRIVIA

nion Major General Edwin Vose Sumner was nicknamed "Bull Head" because he claimed that a musket ball once bounced off his head.

After the war at least twenty men swore they were John Wilkes Booth.

An estimated 300 boys, ages 13 years or younger, served in the Union ranks during the war.

On an average day General Grant was said to have smoked about two dozen cigars.

Robert E. Lee had a pet hen which laid an egg under his camp bed each morning.

The 8th Wisconsin had an eagle named "Old Abe" for a mascot. After serving for four years, "Old Abe" had participated in 42 battles, was wounded once, and finally "retired."

> *"One hole in the seat of the breeches indicates a Captain, two holes a Lieutenant, and the seat all out indicates the individual is a Private."*
> **~Confederate soldier, June 1864**

COFFEE

Maxwell House coffee got its name when a grocer by the name of Joel Cheek developed a special coffee blend, which became popular at the Maxwell House Hotel. After President Theodore Roosevelt was served a cup in 1907, he announced, "It's good to the last drop." The rest is history.

Anyone caught drinking coffee in Turkey in the 16th and 17th centuries was put to death.

If you drink a bubble in your coffee, you will receive money. (Kentucky)

If you want your dreams to come true, don't drink coffee the next morning. (Texas)

To tell your fortune, name the four corners of a lump of sugar and slowly put it into a cup of coffee. (Kentucky)

"Drink coffee and you will be ugly."

The only thing you'll get if you give black coffee to a drunk is a wide-awake drunk!

JERK COFFEE

Stanley Hicks, an old-time banjo and dulcimer maker from Watauga County, North Carolina, swore this story was the gospel truth. There was an old farmer who was the stingiest man that he had ever known. Since coffee was one of the few things you couldn't grow in the mountains of North Carolina, the old man tried to make what little coffee he had last a long time. He used to drill holes in the beans and thread a string through each bean. To make his coffee, he'd dip his string of beans in a cup of hot water, like you would a tea bag, and then jerk it out, hence "jerk coffee." When someone asked Stanley Hicks what *he* called "jerk coffee," his answer was simple: "water."

Two old friends were drinking coffee at a diner. The first man said, "There used to be a waitress here who served me a cup of coffee so weak that she had to help it out of the pot!" The other man said, "That's nuthin'! One time she poured me a cup of coffee so strong, the spoon was standing straight up in the middle of the cup! I couldn't drink it. All I could do was sorta chew on it."

CORN

An ear of corn almost always contains an even number of rows — either twelve, fourteen or sixteen. An ear with an odd number of rows is almost as rare as hen's teeth.

"It takes two to plant corn in Arkansas. One pries the rocks apart with a crowbar and the other fires the seed down the crack with a syringe." *Three Years in Arkansas* by Marion Hughes, 1904.

One farmer's corn crop was so bad that in one meal, he ate fourteen acres of corn!

It's Time to Plant Corn

When you can lay naked on the ground and not feel the cold.

When white oak leaves are as big as a squirrel's ear.

A blue-spotted ear found at a corn husking bee is called a "skew ball" and brings good luck.

CORN

Rural communities commonly held corn shuckings as a way to turn the drudgery of shucking huge quantities of corn into a festive occasion. The entire community was invited and a jug of whiskey was often hidden in the center of the huge pile of corn. The first one to find the jug got the first drink. If a boy found a red ear of corn, he got to kiss the girl of his choice, if he could catch her. Many boys were notorious for sneaking red ears in their pockets.

If the brim of a farmer's hat is turned up, he has corn for sale. (Kentucky)

Grits are sometimes known as "Georgia ice cream."

A cowboy had just returned from many months on the hot dusty trail. He had a powerful thirst, which he aimed to quench. He soon visited every saloon he could find and was about to drink the town dry.

At the end of the night when he was completely plastered, he had gotten into a fight and was last seen flying head first out the swinging doors of a rowdy frontier saloon. He hit the ground with an awful thump, and the nearest man approached him and asked, "Are you hurt?" "No, I ain't hurt," he sobbed. "I'd just like to meet the guy that moved my horse!"

The Pony Express once recruited riders with this advertisement:

"Wanted — Young skinny wiry fellows not over 18. Must be expert riders willing to risk death daily. Orphans preferred. Wages, $25 a week."

Cowboy Wisdom: Only a fool argues with a skunk, a mule or a cook.

COWBOY COOKING LINGO

Axle grease: butter
Bait: food
Bean master: cook
Bear sign: doughnuts
Belly robber: cook
Biscuit: saddle horn
Black water: coffee
Boggy top: a pie with no top crust
Brown gargle: coffee
Bug juice: whiskey
Calf slobber: meringue
Can openers: spurs
Chuck: food
Chuck wagon chicken: bacon
Coosie: cook
Cow salve: butter
Crumb castle: chuck wagon
Dough gods: biscuits
Eatin' irons: knives, forks, spoons
Hot rock: a biscuit
Mexican strawberries: dried beans
Neck oil: whiskey
Pot rustler: cook
Wasp nest: white bread
Put on the nose bag: to eat
Whistle berries: beans

Recipe for Cowboy Coffee

Put 2 lbs of Arbuckle's coffee in a pot with enough water to wet it down. Boil for two hours, then drop in a horse shoe. When the horse shoe floats, the coffee's ready.

COWS

Udder Nonsense

A bug flew into a cow's ear during milking. Not a minute later, the bug squirted out into the milk bucket. In one ear and out the udder.

That Depends...

While driving his shiny new motor car down a country road, a city man struck a cow that was crossing the road. He noticed a farmhouse nearby, so he knocked on the door. A farmer came to the door and the city man asked him how much the cow that was grazing near the road was worth. The

farmer grew pensive and then said, "That all depends on whether you're the tax assessor or whether you just hit her with your car."

To tell where the cows are grazing, hold a daddy-long legs and ask where the cows are. The spider will lift one leg and point in the direction of the cows.

The Talking Heifer

ne day a farmer noticed an ad in a mail order catalog for a course in ventriloquism, so he decided to order it. When the book arrived, the farmer studied it diligently. When his lazy hired hand came to work the next day, the farmer thought he'd play a trick on him. While the hired hand was in the barn milking, the farmer snuck into one of the stalls and waited. After a minute, the heifer seemed to turn her head and then in a clear voice said, *"Ouch! Let go of that hind tit!"*

The hired hand thought he was imagining things, so he kept right on milking. A second later, the heifer raised her voice a little and seem to say, *"You heard me the first time. LET GO!"* With that, the hired hand leaped off his stool and ran out the barn door.

In a few minutes, the hired hand found the farmer and said, "I'm quittin'!" The farmer asked him what was wrong, and the hired hand replied, "If that heifer tells you anything about me, it's a dern lie!"

DIETING, COUNTRY STYLE

The Duct Tape Diet

Determined to lose some weight, a chubby country woman went to the hardware store for some duct tape. Thinking she was fixing her heater, the clerk asked if she also needed some stove pipe. "No thanks," she replied, "the tape is part of my diet plan." The clerk was surprised and silently wondered if she was planning on duct taping her mouth shut. Right then the lady spoke up and said, "I'm gonna duct tape the refrigerator so I can't get the door open!"

$55

More people are poisoned by foul Refrigerators than by sewer gas. Three-fourths of Refrigerators sold breed malaria and fevers, by tainting the food. My **No. 50** House, Hotel and Restaurant Refrigerator will **keep anything** sweet and good. Price **$55** at any R. R. Station in the U. S. Send for Circulars. **B. A. STEVENS, Toledo, Ohio.**

Ice Box, 1882

A man lamented to his friend about his wife's cooking. "Her food is so bad," the man said, "that we pray *after* we eat."

Eat all you can, and can what you can't.

Popular Dieting Myths

Hanging out with really fat people makes you look thinner.

If no one sees you eating, the calories don't count.

Breaking up cookies and eating the pieces burns up lots of calories.

Food licked off knives and forks contains no calories.

Any food you eat in the movies doesn't count after they turn the lights out.

Adding hot sauce to your food makes the pounds "burn off."

If the person you're with eats more than you do, your calories don't count.

When you eat standing up, you burn off more calories than you consume.

DOGS

While on his route, a mailman saw a boy and a huge dog. The mailman asked the boy, "Does your dog bite?" "No sir!" replied the boy. No sooner than the words had left the boy's mouth, the dog bit the mailman right on the leg. The mailman yelled, "I thought you said your dog doesn't bite!" "He doesn't," replied the boy, "That's not my dog!"

An ad appeared in the local paper:

LOST DOG
Reward offered. Missing a leg, an ear, and part of its tail. Answers to the name of "Lucky."

A preacher walked up on four boys who were gathered around a stray dog. "What are you boys doin'?" asked the preacher. "Oh we're seein' who can tell the biggest lie," answered  one of the boys. "The one who tells the biggest whopper gets to keep the dog." The preacher looked shocked and said, "Now, boys, when I was your age I would never think of telling a lie." After a moment of silence, one of the boys said, "Mister, you just got yourself a dog!"

DOGS

A farmer went into the bank to apply for a loan. His dog dutifully sat on the curb outside the bank and waited for him. When the banker refused to grant the loan, the farmer opened the door and started to leave. Right then, his dog ran inside and bit the banker on the leg. Then the dog ran over to one of the bank tellers and bit her too.

Still holding his leg, the banker asked the farmer, "I can understand why your dog would bit me, but why in the world did he bite my bank teller too?" The farmer answered, "To get the bad taste out of his mouth."

"My dog never met a man he didn't lick."

Dog Superstitions

To quiet a howling dog at night, turn a shoe upside down. (Texas)

To find a lost dog, yell through a knothole and the dog will come home.

45

John Quincy Adams

While skinny-dipping in the Potomac, President John Quincy Adams once had his clothes stolen. He finally managed to get a passing boy to go to the White House for more clothes.

Thomas Jefferson

During his eight years as President, Thomas Jefferson and his guests consumed $10,858 in wine. Before he died, Jefferson composed his own epitaph but neglected to mention that he had been two-term President of the United States!

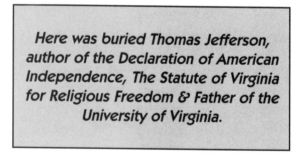

Here was buried Thomas Jefferson, author of the Declaration of American Independence, The Statute of Virginia for Religious Freedom & Father of the University of Virginia.

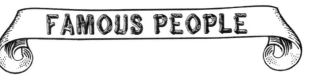
Alexander Hamilton

The first Secretary of the Treasury, Alexander Hamilton, was in debt when he was killed in a duel with Aaron Burr.

William Henry Harrison

The prize for the shortest term for a U.S. President goes to William Henry Harrison. He caught a cold at his inauguration on March 4, 1841 and died 31 days later.

John Tyler

Vice-President John Tyler was down on his knees playing marbles when he heard the news that President William Henry Harrison had died.

Benjamin Franklin

Benjamin Franklin, famous for his expression "A penny saved is a penny earned," was overdrawn on his bank account at least three times each week.

Andrew Jackson

Andrew Jackson once told a friend he never thought much of a man who could think of only one way to spell a word.

FAMOUS PEOPLE

Andrew Johnson

Andrew Johnson, who became President when Lincoln was assassinated, never attended a day of school. His wife taught him to read and write. She was the only First Lady known to have smoked a pipe.

Johnson was the only American President who himself had been a "slave." As a young man, Johnson had been an indentured servant who had run away. Newspaper advertisements appeared in newspapers to try to get him back, but he was never caught.

Horace Greeley

Although Horace Greeley was credited with the phrase "Go West, young man," it was John Soule who first wrote it in an 1851 article for Greeley's publication, "The New Yorker."

Ulysses S. Grant

President Ulysses S. Grant was stopped for speeding in his carriage at the capital. Grant was taken to police headquarters where charges were dropped.

Beyond intending to murder President Lincoln, John Wilkes Booth also had plans to shoot General Grant. The General and his wife had been invited to join the Lincolns at the Ford Theater but they declined the invitation in order to visit their children's school in New Jersey.

National Archives

President Ulysses S. Grant refused to allow his wife to have surgery to correct her cross-eyed vision because he liked her that way.

"I only know two tunes. One is 'Yankee Doodle' and the other isn't."
~Ulysses S. Grant

Theodore Roosevelt

President Theodore Roosevelt was the first President to submerge in a submarine, the U.S.S. *Plunger.* He did it to attract attention away from stalled peace talks between Japan and Russia. His scheme worked, and Roosevelt eventually won the Nobel Peace Prize for brokering the Portsmouth Peace Treaty.

Talk about being tough! After being shot by an insane saloon keeper in 1912, Roosevelt insisted on finishing his speech even while "bleeding like a wounded bull moose." Only when he finished speaking did he accept medical treatment.

Theodore Roosevelt was the first U.S. President to fly in an airplane and the first to ride in an automobile.

The Rough Riders' horses were mistakenly left behind during the Spanish American War, so Roosevelt and his men were forced to fight on foot.

FAMOUS PEOPLE

Calvin Coolidge

Known as a practical joker, Calvin Coolidge liked to push all the buttons on his desk just to see his aides all run in his office at once.

Coolidge was so controlling that he even took over all his wife's duties as First Lady. The President himself supervised housekeeping and menus at the White House. The First Lady even had to get the President's approval before she could buy clothes for herself!

COOLIDGEISMS

"The man who builds a factory builds a temple. And the man who works there worships there."

"When more and more people are thrown out of work, unemployment results."

"No one ever listened themselves out of a job."

"If you don't say anything, you won't be called on to repeat it."

William Howard Taft

At 332 lbs on his inaugural day in 1909, William Howard Taft was America's portliest President. He once got stuck in the bathtub in the White House and had to be pried out by his staff. Soon after, a special tub was ordered for the White House. When it arrived, the four workmen who installed it could easily fit inside it.

In 1910, President Taft got up to stretch during the seventh inning of a baseball game between Philadelphia and Washington. Thinking he was leaving, the crowd stood up to pay him respect, and the seventh inning stretch was born.

President William Howard Taft was a seventh cousin twice removed of Richard M. Nixon, and was a distant relative of Ralph Waldo Emerson. He was once offered a contract to pitch for the Cincinnati Reds.

Henry Ford

Henry Ford was an avid Jews harp player and rarely, if ever, went anywhere without one in his pocket. When he died, all they found on him was a comb, a pocket knife and a Jews harp.

Henry Ford once received this testimonial from the bank robber Clyde Barrow ("Bonnie & Clyde"):

"I drove Fords exclusively when I could get away with one. For sustained speed and freedom from trouble, the Ford has got every other car skinned."

Sears Motor Buggy - $395
12-horse power 2-cylinder engine

Woodrow Wilson

To save money during the First World War, Woodrow Wilson's wife bought a flock of sheep to keep the White House lawn trimmed. She auctioned the wool and gave the $100,000 proceeds to the Red Cross.

George Bernard Shaw

George Bernard Shaw was delivering a lecture when an irate woman stood up and said, "If you were my husband, I'd poison you!" Shaw reportedly replied, "Madame, if I were your husband, I'd take poison!"

Eugene Debs

The only man to run for President while in prison was Eugene Debs. During World War I, he was sent to prison for sedition. Running on the Socialist ticket, he received a million votes, or 3.5% of the total votes cast.

Cole Younger

After serving twenty-five years in prison, famed outlaw Cole Younger joined ex-outlaw Frank Ford on the lecture circuit to warn the public against the evils of crime. Finally, they made crime pay.

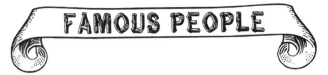

FAMOUS PEOPLE

W.C. Fieldisms

"Anyone who hates dogs and children can't be all bad."

"There's no such thing as a tough child — if you parboil them first for seven hours, they always come out tender."

"Drink is your enemy — love your enemies."

"I am free of prejudice. I hate everyone equally."

"Somebody left the cork out of my lunch."

"Start off every day with a smile and get it over with."

"I never drink water — look at the way it rusts pipes."

"If at first you don't succeed, try, try again. Then quit. No use being a damn fool about it."

> *Despite W.C. Fields' image of hating children, he willed a large portion of his estate to start an orphanage.*

Al Caponeisms

"When I sell liquor, it's called bootlegging; when my patrons serve it on Lake Shore Drive, it's called 'hospitality.'"

"You can get much farther with a kind word and a gun than you can with a kind word alone."

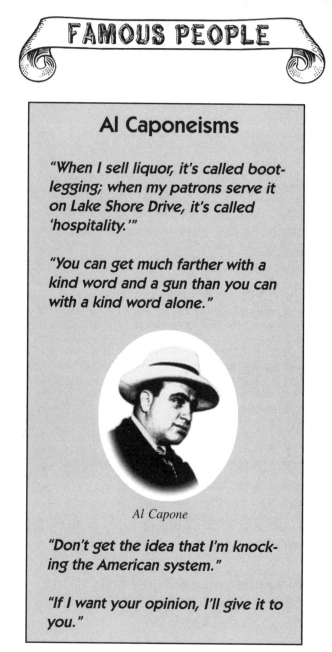

Al Capone

"Don't get the idea that I'm knocking the American system."

"If I want your opinion, I'll give it to you."

Lyndon B. Johnson

Lyndon B. Johnson once accused Gerald Ford of playing "too much football with his helmet off."

On a rural road a state trooper pulled over a farmer and said, "Sir, did you know that your wife fell out of your truck several miles back?" "Thank God!" replied the farmer. "I thought I had gone deaf."

That's Once

A farmer and his new bride were returning home from their wedding in their wagon. All of a sudden, their old horse stumbled and the farmer said, "That's once." A little further down the road, the old horse stumbled

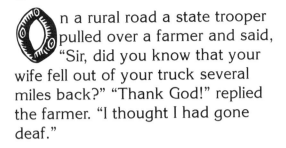

again, and the farmer said, "That's twice." Pretty soon the old horse stumbled yet again. This time the farmer didn't say anything, but reached under the seat, pulled out a shotgun and shot the horse. His new bride turned to him and said, "What did you go and kill the horse for?"

The farmer then said, *"That's once."*

The Mud Hole

While driving down a country lane, a man and wife drove through a mud hole and their car became hopelessly mired. After trying to get the car out by themselves, they saw a farmer driving some oxen down the road. When he saw their predicament, the farmer stopped and  offered to pull their car out of the mud for $5. The couple agreed and minutes later their car was free.

As he was leaving, the farmer said, "You know, you're the tenth car I've pulled out of the mud today." The husband then asked, "When do you have time to plow your land? At night?" "No," the farmer replied, "Night is when I put the water in the hole."

An ardent Believer, one farmer named his five children Matthew, Mark, Luke, Ann, John.

FARMERS

The Amazing Talking Bull

An insurance salesman from a big city decided to drum up some business out in the country. He cranked up his car and drove out to a rural area. All of a sudden the engine of his car quit running. Knowing almost nothing about cars, he opened up the hood and looked helplessly inside. From behind him, he heard a deep voice that said, "It's the carburetor."

The insurance man looked around, but there was no one there. Turning his attention back under the hood, he soon heard the voice again, "It's the carburetor." Looking around, all he could see was a large Brahma bull standing behind him. Scared out of his wits, he took off running to a farm house that was about a half mile away.

He arrived at the farmhouse and frantically knocked on the door. When the farmer appeared, the man explained the situation. The farmer asked, "Was there a big Brahma bull nearby?" The man shook his head and said, "Yes, yes, there was!" The farmer laughed and said, "Just ignore that bull. He doesn't know as much about cars as he thinks he does."

FARMERS

What Are You Worth?

One time a farmer hired a day laborer to help dig potatoes. "What'll ya pay me, Sir?" asked the laborer. "Why, I'll pay you exactly what you're worth," answered the farmer. The laborer put down his hoe and said, "Sir, I don't believe I can work for that."

A backwoods farmer was approached by a state agricultural agent who was trying to tell him about the newest kind of hog feed. "It will reduce the time it takes to get your hogs to market," said the agent. The farmer looked at the agent in disbelief and said, "What's time to a hog?"

Farming Superstitions

Redheaded farmers raise more carrots than anyone else, and the best red peppers. (Texas)

FARMERS

A Texan in Australia

A Texas farmer took a long-awaited vacation to Australia. There he met a local farmer who showed off his wheat field. The Texan boasted, "We have wheat fields so big they'll make yours look like a postage stamp." Then they walked around the ranch and the Australian showed off a pasture with a herd of cattle grazing. The Texan said, "We have cattle ranches so big they'll make yours look like an ant colony." Finally, the Texan saw a herd of kangaroos hopping through the field. "What in the heck are those?" asked the Texan. The Australian farmer turned to the Texan and said, "Don't you have any grasshoppers in Texas?"

What did the disgruntled pig say to the farmer? "You take me for grunted."

That Ain't Bull

After his prized bull was run over by a train, an old farmer filed suit against the railroad. The court finally awarded the farmer half the value of the bull.

After the trial, the lawyer who had defended the railroad shared the elevator with the old farmer who had filed the suit. "You know, old man," said the lawyer, "I couldn't have won the case. The engineer was asleep at the switch and the fireman was drunk in the caboose when the train hit your bull. I didn't have a single witness to put on the stand. I bluffed you!"

The old farmer looked surprised, but replied, "Well, I'll tell you one thing young feller. I had my doubt about winning the case after the bull came home this morning."

FESTIVALS

The Great Outhouse Blowout

hatever you do, don't miss the Great Outhouse Blowout. This festival is held in Gravel Switch, Kentucky, on the first Saturday in October at an 1850s country store. Be sure to sign up for the competition known as "The Outhouse 300." For this contest, five-member teams push and pull their "designer outhouses" on wheels over the 300 foot course to try to win the grand prize in outhouse racing. Good luck!

Penn Store, 257 Penn's Store Rd., Gravel Switch, KY 40328, www.pennstore.com (859) 332-7715

The Woolly Worm Festival

With the slogan "Hey, you woolly ought to be there!" the Banner Elk Chamber of Commerce holds the annual **Woolly Worm Festival** every October in the mountains of western North Carolina. The highlight of the festival is the race where woolly worms compete for cash and prestige. The winner is examined by festival forecasters who pronounce the official winter weather forecast based on the coloration of the victorious caterpillar.

For information, contact www.chamber@averycounty.com

Chitlin' Strut

From the self-declared "Chitlin' Capital of the World," Salley, South Carolina, comes the annual Chitlin' Strut held the first Saturday after Thanksgiving.

For this event, the town of Salley trucks in 8000 lbs. of chitlins, 1000 lbs. of flour, 175 gallons of peanut oil, 94 lbs. of hot sauce, 150 loaves of bread and 750 lbs. of ice. If you can tear yourself away from a plate of chitlins, you can enter the hog calling contest or the beauty pageant.

For information, contact the town of Salley, S.C. (838) 258-3485

Mule Day

On the first Saturday of November, judges in Calvary, Georgia, cast their vote for "The Ugliest Mule," "The Prettiest Mule," and the "Most Stubborn Mule." There's also a mule parade, plus plowing, cane-grinding, syrup-making, and greased pig chasing. Don't miss the mule race where handlers try to outdo each other trying to get their stubborn mules to move.

FESTIVALS

Annual Rattlesnake Derby

One of the strangest festivals of them all is the Annual Rattlesnake Derby, held each April in Mangum, Oklahoma. Now in its 36th year, it is the biggest festival in Oklahoma. After a first-aid and safety briefing, snake hunters caravan to designated areas where they actually get out and hunt live rattlesnakes! At the end of the festival, a "Snake of the Day" award is presented. There are also prizes for "Most Snakes," "Most Pounds," and "Longest Snake." In case of a dispute, a Fangmaster decides who wins.

The longest snake taken so far was in 1997 when someone caught a diamondback rattler measuring 84". In another hunt, a man caught 899½ lbs of snakes! Not to be outdone, in the 1984 contest, a snake hunter caught 381 rattlesnakes on a single day!

If you're too squeamish to enter the rattlesnake derby, you can participate in the rattlesnake dance or you can enter the beauty contest in which they crown "Miss Derby."

For more information, you can contact the Shortgrass Rattlesnake Assoc., Inc., 222 W. Jefferson, Magnum, OK 73554 (580) 782-2434

Cow Chip Championship

f you're in Beaver, Oklahoma in April, don't miss this festival. So you can start practicing, here are some of the official rules:

1. Two chips per contestant. The chip thrown the farthest shall be the only one counted. If the chip breaks up in mid-air during the throw, the piece going the farthest will be counted.

2. Chips shall be at least six inches in diameter.

3. Contestants must select their own chips from the wagon load provided by the committee.

4. Decision of the Judge is final.

The best score in the men's cow chip throwing contest is Leland Searcy's 1979 toss of 182 feet, 3 inches. In 1989, Kay Hankins from Prairie Du Sac, Wisconsin threw her cow chip a record 132 feet.

When I told my wife Barbara to start practicing, she said she only wanted to throw cow chips at me!

Contact the Beaver C of C
PO Box 878, Beaver, Oklahoma 73932
(580) 625-4726

FESTIVALS

Mike the Headless Chicken

No, we didn't dream this one up; this is an actual festival held the third weekend of May in Fruita, Colorado. The story begins back in 1945 when Lloyd and Clara Olsen selected a rooster named Mike to be the guest of honor for supper. Lloyd grabbed Mike in one hand and an axe in the other and wop! Off went Mike's head. But to Lloyd's surprise, being headless didn't seem to slow Mike up one bit.

Lloyd and Clara were used to head-less chickens run-ning around for a short while after they had been beheaded. But Mike just kept right on living like nothing was wrong. They did have to feed him with an eye dropper, but except for that, Mike was like any other red blooded rooster. The only thing they noticed he couldn't do was crow!

When scientists examined Mike, they found that the axe had not quite chopped off Mike's entire head. It missed the jugular vein and left un-touched the brain stem, which controls most of a chicken's important functions.

Lloyd and Clara were soon calling Mike the Miracle Chicken! Since you can't keep a miracle quiet, word about Mike the Headless Chicken quickly spread. It wasn't long before a huckster named Hope Wade approached the Olsens about cashing in on Mike's growing fame. They soon had Mike touring nationally in a circus sideshow as "Mike the Wonder Chicken." People flocked to see him and willingly paid 25 cents a peek. At the height of his fame, Miracle Mike was raking in $4500 a week, not exactly chicken feed! He was valued and insured for $10,000.

Mike's show business career came to a screeching halt in March of 1947 when he was accidentally killed by his owners while they were staying at a Phoenix motel. Though he passed on to the chicken ranch in the sky, Mike's record of living without a head for eighteen months will no doubt be a hard act to follow.

But even in death, Mike is fondly remembered at the Fruita festival that includes a Headless Chicken Race, egg toss, Pin the Head on the chicken, and even a Chicken Cluck-Off.

For information, call the Fruita Recreation Department at (970)858-0360.

FINGERNAIL LORE

The number of white spots on a girl's fingernails tells the number of boyfriends or children she will have.

Cut Fingernails on:

Monday for health
Tuesday for wealth
Wednesday is the best day of all
Thursday for losses
Friday for crosses
Saturday for no luck at all
Sunday you pare nails for evil
And all the week you'll be ruled by
the devil.

If you cut your fingernails on Friday, you'll never have a toothache.

If you cut your fingernails on Sunday, you will have a shamed face before Monday.

FIDDLING AROUND

Fiddle Tune Names

Devil Was a Whittler
Devil Ate the Groundhog
Everybody Knows What Maggie Done
Forty-Eight Dogs in the Meat House
Good for the Tongue Hornpipe
Hell to Pay in Tulsa
Indian Ate the Woodchuck
Jenny Run Away in the Mud in the
      Night
John Newgrant Came Home with a
      Pain in His Head
Josie Shuck Her Pants Down
Maggots in the Sheep's Hide
Monkey on the Dog Cart
More Holler Than Wool
Nail That Catfish to a Tree
Push the Pig's Foot a Little Closer to
      the Fire
Sal's Got Mud Between Her Toes
Sheep Shell Corn by the Rattling of
      His Horn
That's My Rabbit, My Dog Caught It
The Pretty Little Girl Went to Texas
      and Fell in a Well
The Hog Went Through the Fence,
      Yoke and All
The Tune the Old Cow Died Of
The Old Cow Died in the Forks of the
      Branch
Where's My Other Foot?
Who Hit Nellie with the Stove Pipe?
Who Throwed Lye on My Dog?
You Married My Daughter But Yet You
      Didn't

FIDDLING AROUND

A man went into a fiddle shop to buy a string for his fiddle. The fiddle master had gone out, and a young boy was left to watch the shop in his absence. "I'd like to buy an E string please," but the boy thought he said a "He" string. The boy rustled around in the box of strings and finally looked up and shrugged. "How do you tell the 'He' strings from the 'She' strings?"

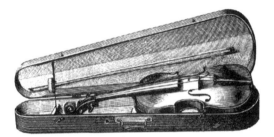

Definition of a fiddle: An instrument to tickle human ears by friction of a horse's tail on the entrails of a cat.

"He fiddles like the strings are still in the cat!"

"It takes more than a white hat and a flashy belt buckle to play the fiddle." ~Jim Shumate, fiddler

FISHING LORE

Grandpa and the Game Warden

Far be it for me to call my grandfather lazy. Let's just call him "ingenious." Instead of sitting with a pole and can of bait for hours on end, he liked to fish with a stick of dynamite. When the fish came floating to the top, Grandpa scooped 'em up with a net and went on his merry way.

When the game warden heard about Grandpa's fishing habits, he paid him a friendly visit. Grandpa offered to take him along and show him his fishing techniques. As soon as they got out on the lake, Grandpa handed the warden a stick of dynamite and then struck a match to the fuse. With only a second before the thing went off, the warden got rid of it in a hurry by tossing it as far as he could in the lake. After Grandpa had gathered up the fish, they made a deal. The warden wouldn't press charges if Grandpa kept it secret who threw the dynamite in the lake.

A salesman knocked on the door of a farm house and asked the lady of the house if her husband was in. "He's gone fishing," she said. "If you want to find him, just go down to the fork in the creek. There you'll find a pole with a worm on each end."

FISHING LORE

Behold the fisherman

e riseth early in the morning and disturbeth the whole household. Mighty are his prospects. He goeth forth full of hope. And when the day is far spent he returneth, smelling of strong drink; and the truth is not in him.

A Big Baby

When President Cleveland's second child was born, the doctor asked the proud father to bring him a scale so that he could weigh the new offspring. Cleveland went down in the cellar and brought up a scale, which he used to weigh the fish he caught on his numerous trips. When they placed the child on the scale, the infant weighed 35 pounds!

In Oklahoma, it is against the law to get a fish drunk.

Fooling the Game Warden

A testy old fisherman was walking along a trail decked out in his waders, creel, net, hat and pole when the game warden spotted him. The warden said, "Let me see your fishing license." The old guy just kept on walking, but replied over his shoulder, "I ain't fishin'."

The warden followed him to the banks of the river and again said, "Let me see your fishing license," but the old man replied, "I ain't fishin'."

Not one to give up easily, the game warden finally tracked the old fisherman to the middle of a wide river. This time, the old man called out, "Come on out and check my license. "Now I'm fishin'."

One fisherman told his buddy, "Yesterday I caught a rainbow trout that was a yard long, and that's the truth!" His friend shot right back, "Well, yesterday when I went fishing, I hooked a lantern at the bottom of the pond, and it was still lit!" The first man then suggested a compromise: "If you'll blow out that lantern, I'll saw a foot or two off of that trout!"

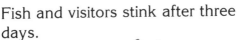

Fish and visitors stink after three days.

If you count the number of fish you have caught, you will catch no more fish that day.

Fish wouldn't get hooked if they kept their mouths shut.

While you are fishing, name the worm. If you catch a fish your lover is true. (Kentucky)

Eating fish heads will make you smart. (Texas)

I ask a simple question:
An answer I surely wish:
Are all fisherman liars
Or do all the liars fish?

When the wind's in the east
The trout bite least,
When the wind's in the west
The trout bite best.

The fishing was so bad, even the liars weren't catching anything.

One fisherman swore the fish he caught was so big that just the shadow weighed 14 pounds.

GENERAL STORES

Too Many Nuts

Two old codgers were sitting on the front porch of a general store. One had just bought a candy bar and was unwrapping it. The other fellow started talking about a few of the books he'd read when he was a young man. "Do you like O. Henry?" he asked. The old codger with the candy bar turned to his friend and replied, "I can't eat 'em any more, too many nuts."

Country Inflation

A lady was squeezing all the tomatoes and finally approached the grouchy grocer and asked, "How much are these tomatoes?" He frowned and said, "Thirty-five cents a pound." She then asked, "Did you raise them yourself?" "Yes," he said. "They were thirty cents a pound yesterday."

The Old-Timer

An old man with a long white beard was sitting on the front stairs of a general store. A tourist came along and greeted the old man with, "Say, old timer, tell me how old are you?"

The old man looked surprised and replied, "I'm just a hundred." The tourist said, "Well, I doubt that you'll see another hundred." With that, the old man said, "I ain't so sure about that. I'm stronger now than when I started my first hundred."

No Justice

A farmer and a grocer were talking politics over a game of checkers. "There is no justice in this world," said the farmer. "The rich man can buy all he wants on credit, but the poor man must pay for everything in cash. It should be the rich who pay cash, and the poor who should be able to buy on credit."

"That sounds well and good in theory," said the grocer, "but if I were to extend credit to all the loafers in this town, I'd soon be poor myself." "Then you'd have nothing to worry about," said the farmer. "You'd be able to get everything on credit!"

Silence is Golden

A newcomer decided to hang out with the loafers on the porch of a general store in Maine. He sat there and sat there, and nobody said anything. Finally, he asked, "Is there a law against talking in this town?" "Oh no," answered one of the locals. "We just have an understanding that unless you can improve on silence, you should keep still!"

The above story reminds me of the only thing I can still remember from my 10th grade English class. My teacher's theory was that people in cold climates talk less than people in warmer climates. "Why?" you ask. Because they didn't want all that cold air getting in their mouths!

He Was a Her

Charlie Parkhurst was one of the roughest, toughest stagecoach drivers of the Gold Rush days. But "Charlie" turned out to be a woman! Her true gender was revealed only when she was being dressed for burial. In her prime, Charlie could drink, smoke cigars, chew tobacco and cuss with the best of the male drivers.

On August 3, 1849, a thirsty prospector paid fifteen dollars for a glass of water and another paid one hundred dollars for a pint of water.

In 1849 in California, chickens sold for 16 dollars each, and eggs were fifty cents a piece.

During the Gold Rush, an ounce of gold could be redeemed for about sixteen dollars. That was the same as the cost of a pound of gun powder or a bottle of champagne.

GRANDDAD IN THE OUTHOUSE

One of my bygone recollections,
As I recall the days of yore
Is the little house, behind the house,
With the crescent over the door.

'Twas a place to sit and ponder
With your head bowed down low;
Knowing that you wouldn't be there,
If you didn't have to go.

You had to make these frequent trips
Whether snow, rain, sleet, or fog—
To the little house where you usually
Found the Sears-Roebuck catalog.

Oft times in dead of winter,
The seat was covered with snow.
'Twas then with much reluctance,
To the little house you'd go.

I recall the day Granddad,
Who stayed with us one summer,
Made a trip to the shanty
Which proved to be a hummer.

'Twas the same day my Dad
Finished painting the kitchen green.
He'd just cleaned up the mess he'd made
With rags and gasoline.

He tossed the rags in the shanty hole
And went on his usual way
Not knowing that by doing so
He would certainly rue the day.

GRANDDAD IN THE OUTHOUSE
(CONTINUED)

Now Granddad had an urgent call,
I never will forget!
This trip he made to the little house
Lingers in my memory yet.

He sat down on the shanty seat,
With both feet on the floor.
Then filled his pipe with tobacco
And struck a match on the door.

After the tobacco began to glow,
He slowly raised his rear
Tossed the match in the open hole,
With no concern or fear.

The blast that followed, I am sure
Was heard for miles around;
And there was poor ol' Granddad
Just sitting on the ground.

The smoldering pipe still in his mouth,
His suspenders he held tight;
The celebrated three-holer
Was blown clear out of sight.

When asked him what had happened,
His answer I'll never forget.
He thought it must be something
That he had recently et!

Next day we had a new one,
Which my Dad built with ease.
With a sign on the entrance door
Which read, "No Smoking, Please!"

81

"Here lies my wife, here let her lie
Now she has peace, and so do I.
I laid my wife beneath this stone
For her repose and for my own."

"Here lies an Atheist
All dressed up
And no place to go!"
(Thurmont, Maryland)

"On the 22nd of June
Jonathan Fiddle
Went out of tune."
(Hartscombe, England)

"I told you I was sick!"
(Round Rock, TX)

"Here lies Lester Moore
Four slugs from a .44
No Les No More."
Boot Hill Cemetery, Tombstone, Az.

"On the whole, I'd rather be in Philadelphia." W.C. Fields

"Here lies Butch.
We planted him raw.
He was quick on the trigger,
But slow on the draw."
(Silver City, Nevada)

"Here Lies Mary Smith
Silent At Last"

"He died at a public gathering
When the platform
Suddenly gave away."

"Here lies Johnny Yeast
Pardon me for not rising."
(Ruidoso, N. M.)

"Don't believe everything you read on tombstones." (Texas saying)

The First Auto

While hoeing corn, a farmer and his son heard a strange noise coming up the road. Surely it was the end of the world. The farmer told his son, "Run and get me my gun." The younger man took off running and came back in a few minutes with a shotgun, which he handed to his father. Right then, the "thing" rounded a curve and came into full view. The farmer fired a warning shot, and the "thing" came to a sudden stop. A man jumped out and started yelling. The farmer and his son couldn't hear what the man was yelling, but the son looked over at his father and asked, "Did you kill it, Pa?" The farmer replied, "I don't believe I killed it, but it sure let go of that man!"

His First Phone Call

Homer Mullinix had never used a telephone. On a rare trip to town he worked up his nerve and decided he would try using one. With a little help he managed to dial over to the general store, where his wife was buying groceries. At that very instant, lightning struck the phone wire, and Homer let go of the phone in a hurry. "That was her, all right!"

The Census Taker

An old mountain man was sitting on his rocker on the front porch of his cabin when up rode a census taker. "Good day, Sir," said the census taker. "I'm here to take the census. How many children do you have?"

The old man thought for a minute and finally said, "My girls are named Tildy, Bertie, Lessie, Bessie, Ottie, Dora, Ollie, Hessie, and Pearlie. My boys we call Claude, Artle, and Ambrose." "No, you don't understand," said the census taker. "I don't need names, I only need numbers." "Numbers?" asked the surprised old timer. "We ain't run out of names yet!"

Mo' 'lasses

A country girl returned home from college and spent the day with her grannie, who asked, "Honey, do you want 'lasses on your cornbread?"

"Grannie!" said the uppity college girl. "It's not 'lasses; it's pronounced 'mo-lasses.'" The grannie looked surprised, but answered back, "How can you have *mo'* 'lasses, when you ain't had any 'lasses yet?"

When a hill country boy returned home for summer vacation, he tried to impress his father with the big words he had learned. "Yesterday," he told his father, "my friends and I autoed to the drive-in, golfed until dark, bridged for a few hours, then autoed home." "That's wonderful, son. "I muled to the cornfield and gee-hawed 'til sundown, then I suppered 'til dark, piped 'til nine, bedsteaded 'til five, breakfasted and went muling again."

On Christmas eve, a mother was trying to get her excited children to go to bed by telling them stories. "God gave you eyes to see, ears to hear, a nose to smell, and feet to run," she said. Her little girl sat up and said, "Mother, I think God must have got mixed up on brother. His nose runs and his feet smell."

HOBO JOKES

One hobo told his buddy, "I always suspected that smoking was bad for my health, but I didn't know for sure until recently." "What happened recently?" asked his buddy. "I went out to pick up a cigar and someone stepped on my hand."

A hobo was hauled into court, charged with vagrancy. "What's your name?" demanded the judge. "Locke Smith," was the reply as he bolted for the door. He was seized by an officer and brought back. "That'll be ten dollars or ten days," said the magistrate. "Judge, if it's OK with you, I'll take the ten dollars."

One day a hobo came to the door of an old Jewish lady and said, "I haven't eaten in three days." The woman replied, "You must force yourself to eat."

"Were you ever in love or married?" asked one hobo to another. "Yep, I've been in love, but never married. The old gal wouldn't marry me when I was drunk, and I wouldn't marry her when I was sober."

> *Loafing is so exhausting, because you can't quit and rest.*

HOBO SLANG

Balloon: a bindle
Bindle stiff: a hobo carrying a bindle
Biscuit: a one dollar coin
Bone polisher: a mean dog
Buzz: to beg
Croaked gumps: killed chickens
Croaker: a doctor
Deck: to board a train
Dimmer: a dime
Glim: a match or light
Gooseberrying: stealing clothes from
    a clothesline
Graveyard: hash
Growler: a can of beer
Hay bag: a woman on the road
Headlights: eggs
Hit the grit: jump from a moving train
Hog: locomotive
Hooty: angry
Hundred on a plate: baked beans
Jitney: a five cent piece
Jolt wagon: paddy wagon
Lump: a handout
Mulligan: hobo stew
Navy: cigar butt
Nickel flop: all night movie house
Pearl diver: a restaurant dishwasher
Pill-roller: a doctor
Saddle blankets: hot cakes
Sap: a policeman's stick
Side-door pullman: boxcar
Sinker: doughnut
Turkey: US half dollar
Weeds: hobo jungle
West bound: dead
Whiteline: white corn whiskey

HORSE SENSE

A man went to buy a horse for his wife, but soon realized the horse required a stern hand to keep it in line. He finally asked the owner of the horse if he thought it was a suitable horse for his wife. The man paused and then said, "Well, I think a certain type of woman could handle this horse, but I sure wouldn't want to be married to that kind of a woman!"

"Say Farmer, why don't you buy my horse? He goes ten miles without stopping." "That won't work," said the skeptical farmer. "It's only five miles to town. I'd have to walk back five miles every time I rode him."

A man rode his horse into town, arriving on Friday. After three days, he left on Friday. How was that possible? Answer:

His horse's name was Friday.

"Having horse sense doesn't keep a man from behaving like a jackass."

HORSE SENSE

While hoeing corn near a cross roads, a country boy saw a circuit-riding preacher ride up on the sorriest looking horse he had ever seen. The preacher, who was decked out in a forked-tail coat and a wide-brimmed black hat, asked the boy, "Which one of these roads should I take to get to the Methodist church?" The country boy had to stifle a snicker but replied as respectfully as he could, "Sir, it doesn't matter which one of these roads you take, you'll never get there on that horse."

HORSE SUPERSTITION
When horses kick their stalls at night, thieves are nearby.

It is illegal to ride an ugly horse down the street in Wilbur, Washington.

Never ride a horse named "Buck."

HOT & COLD

It was hotter than...

The hinges of hell.
A billy goat in a pepper patch.
A stolen tamale.
A honeymoon hotel.

It was so hot...

The rattlesnakes crawled into a camp
fire and coiled up in the shade
of the coffee pot.
The birds had to use a pot holder to
pull worms out of their holes.
The chickens were plucking themselves.

It was cold as...

A cast-iron commode.
An ex-wife's heart.
A mother-in-law's kiss.
An outhouse seat in winter.
A pawnbroker's smile.
The wart on a well digger's nose.

♪

Many Eskimos use refrigerators to
keep their food from freezing.

♪

The largest hailstone on record fell at
Coffeyville, Kansas in September,
1970. It weighed 1.67 lbs and mea-
sured 12½ inches in circumference.

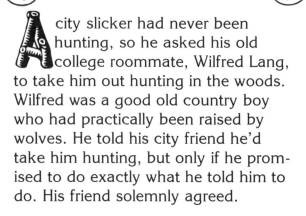

A city slicker had never been hunting, so he asked his old college roommate, Wilfred Lang, to take him out hunting in the woods. Wilfred was a good old country boy who had practically been raised by wolves. He told his city friend he'd take him hunting, but only if he promised to do exactly what he told him to do. His friend solemnly agreed.

Once they got out in the middle of the woods, Wilfred showed his friend how to fire his gun and then gave him these instructions: "Lie down right there on that log 'til I get back and don't move a inch. When a deer comes along, plug him right between the eyes. Until then, **DON'T EVEN MOVE A HAIR!**"

After several hours, Wilfred started to hike back when he heard an awful commotion and saw his friend frantically running toward him. "What in the world is wrong?" asked Wilfred. "When a mountain lion came along and sharpened his claws on the log I was lying on, I didn't move. When a bear came along and sat on the log, I didn't move. And when a rattlesnake came along and slithered over my body, I didn't move. But when I overheard a conversation between two giant mosquitos, I moved.

"What in the world did the mosquitos say?" asked Wilfred. "One of the giant mosquitos asked the other one, 'Should we eat him here, or bring him back home?' The second giant mosquito told him, "Let's eat him here. If we take him home, our older brothers will take him away from us!'"

He's as exciting as a mashed potato sandwich.

He looks like he was gonna clobber up and churn.

He's so stingy he wouldn't give you the air out of a jug.

He don't know gee from haw.

He's all gurgle and no guts.

He's all hat and no hogs.

She's so cross-eyed, when she cries the tears roll down her back.

He's so bowlegged he couldn't stop a pig in a ditch.

He looks like he's been dragged through a brush heap backwards.

He's two pickles short of a picnic.

He's so mean he'd steal the air out of an old lady's tires.

If his brains were dynamite, he couldn't blow his nose.

He's one taco short of a combination plate.

She's got a hole in her screen door.

She was as fat as a #4 washtub.

He's so mean, he'd throw his bath water on an old lady's kindling.

Her biscuits didn't rise.

He sits around like a turd in a dead eddy.

He's so cheap he wouldn't pay to watch an ant pull a freight train up Pike's Peak.

He didn't have both oars in the water.

He's missing a few spokes of his wheel.

She's parked too far from the curb.

The cheese done slid off her cracker.

He's a few fish short of a full stringer.

She don't know turds from mashed potatoes.

She's so ugly...

She looks like she's passing a peach pit.

Her eyes look like two fried eggs in a slop bucket.

Her face looks like it's worn out two bodies.

She's as ugly as home-made soup.

Her eyes look like two rabbit pellets in a snow bank.

She looks like she's been dragged face first through a bed of hot coals.

She has enough chins for three faces.

My gal's so skinny...

You could use her for a dipstick.

She has to run around in the shower to get wet.

She could hide behind a straw.

When she sits on a dollar, ninety cents of it shows.

She could slide down the barrel of a shotgun.

He's so country...

His idea of "dressing up" is wearing clean overalls.

The only time he takes off his hat is when he's getting ready to apologize.

He thought cornbread was wedding cake.

INVENTIONS

The famous inventor, Francis Bacon, was conducting experiments in the snow in 1626 to see if the cold would delay the decomposition of bodies. He then caught cold and died.

Branding cattle was introduced to America by the Spanish conquistador, Hernando Cortez. It proved to be a cheap alternative to building fences.

Matches, once known as "Lucifers," were invented by the Englishman John Walker, who refused to patent his invention because he felt that such an important discovery should belong to the public.

Butter may have been accidentally invented by an anonymous Bedouin tribesman who set out on a long journey with a skin filled with milk strapped to his camel. By the time he reached his destination, the milk had been "churned" into butter.

Potato chips were the 1853 invention of George Crum, a cook at a Saratoga Lake, New York resort. In response to complaints about his thick french fries, he shaved some potatoes paper thin and potato chips were born!

Benjamin Franklin's Inventions: lending library, swim fins, bifocals, the rocking chair, daylight savings time (which didn't begin until World War I).

The fork was invented by the French King, Henry III (1551-1581), to help him eat meat without using his fingers.

Speaking of forks, a fork with a timer was issued U.S. Patent 5,421,089. The fork signals when it's time to take another bite. By slowing down your eating, you presumably eat less. And since your food will likely get cold, it won't be as much fun to eat, so you eat less.

A hat tipper was patented March 10, 1896 that allowed tipping a hat with your hands in your pockets.

BVDs were named in 1876 after the founders of an underwear company, Bradley, Voorhees and Day.

"Everything that can be invented has been invented." **Charles H. Duell, Commissioner, U.S. Office of Patents, 1899.**

John Muir, the famous naturalist, invented a contraption for getting himself out of bed in the morning. His bed was attached to a series of wooden gears. When it was time to rise, his bed tilted, tumbling him on to the floor.

An alarm clock was patented in 1907 that squirted water in the face of the slumbering person.

Jell-O was invented by Peter Cooper, who built America's first passenger locomotive, *Tom Thumb*.

Lincoln Logs were the invention of John Lloyd, the son of Frank Lloyd Wright.

A better mousetrap was patented March 31, 1908. Lured by a piece of cheese, the unsuspecting mouse sticks his head in the trap and suddenly a bell is snapped on his neck. When the unhurt mouse returns to its nest, the ringing bell scares the other mice into fleeing the house.

Iced tea was invented at the 1904 World's Fair in St. Louis. When hot weather ruined his tea business, Englishman Richard Blechynden served his tea over ice, which became an instant hit.

By the time Thomas Edison invented the phonograph, he was almost completely deaf.

THOMAS A. EDISON
1847 - FEB. - 1947

The inventor of the light bulb was afraid of the dark!

The Wall Street Ticker was invented by Edison at the tender age of twenty-three. He was going to ask for $5,000 for his invention, but was afraid that amount was too high. Instead, Edison suggested that the president of the large Wall Street investment house make an offer. After he was offered $40,000, Edison learned the benefits of keeping his mouth shut.

Raisin Bread was invented by Henry David Thoreau.

The Ice Cream Sundae was invented to get around an Illinois law in the 1880s which prohibited the sale of ice-cream sodas on Sunday. The result was a treat served with just ice cream and syrup and named a "Sunday Soda" or "Sundae."

INVENTIONS

Victims of the panic of 1837 included the inventor Cyrus McCormick. Declaring bankruptcy, he lost his farm and most of his belongings. His newly-invented reaper was thought to be worthless, so his creditors let him keep it. We also have McCormick to thank for inventing the installment plan.

ॐ

Bloomers were named after Amelia Jenks Bloomer, who shocked her community by refusing to include the words "promise to obey" in her wedding vows. She started the first woman's magazine.

ॐ

The Telegraph was invented by Samuel F. B. Morse after it took seven days for him to learn of his wife's death by the mail.

Dynamite was invented by Alfred Nobel, who also invented plywood.

ॐ

The yard was originally based on the distance between the nose and the thumb of King Henry I of England.

Missing Persons

 farmer's wife went to the police station to report that her husband was missing. "Can you give me a description of him?" asked the police chief. "Oh yes," she said. "He's short, bald, fat, pigeon-toed, bow legged, and he wears false teeth." "Is there anything you'd like to add to that?" asked the chief. "He wears old clothes, even to church, and he's got a scraggly beard with chewing tobacco stains all over it." Then she paused and said, "Oh, let's just forget the whole thing!"

Good Morning!

A policeman stopped a speeding car that was slow to pull over. "Didn't you hear me say, 'Pull over?'" he asked. "Oh, beg your pardon officer. I thought I heard you say 'Good morning, Mayor!'" The officer's face went white but he managed to reply, "It *is* a nice morning, isn't it?"

★

The number of armed robberies in Iceland in 1990: Zero.

No Hurry

One chilly evening in the early part of March, the sheriff entered the jail cell of a condemned prisoner. "Gabe," the sheriff began. "Tomorrow's your hanging day. What do you want for your last breakfast on earth?" "Sheriff, I'd like to have a nice ripe watermelon," said the prisoner. "But Gabe," said the sheriff, "watermelons won't be ripe for four or five more months yet." "I can wait."

The Fart Law

Backed up with a whopping fine of $100, the Alaska legislature introduced a bill to punish "public flatulence, crepitation, gaseous emission, and miasmic effluence."

Worm Dealer Caught!

Fourteen officers from the Ohio Wildlife Division caught an unlicensed worm dealer red-handed selling worms to undercover agents. The accused "criminal" turned out to be an eight-year-old boy selling worms to a fisherman in his front yard. The case was eventually dismissed and the boy and the worms were let off the hook.

British law in 1845 made it a capital offence to commit suicide. The punishment was death by hanging.

★

Salt Lake City, Utah, has a law against carrying an unwrapped ukulele on the street.

★

In Michigan it is illegal to chain an alligator to a fire hydrant.

★

In Alabama there's a law against wearing a fake moustache that causes laughter in church.

★

The town of Gary, Indiana, once banned eating garlic within four hours of attending the theater.

★

In Portland, Maine, it's a crime for a man to tickle a women under the chin with a feather duster.

★

Salem, Massachusetts, has a law against wearing a goatee without a license.

★

A law in Michigan states that a woman's hair legally belongs to her husband.

★

A woman can't dance on a table in a saloon in Helena, Montana, unless she has on at least 3 lbs. of clothing.

 ew York has a law against flirting in public. A second conviction mandates that horse blinders be worn while out in public.

★

It is against the law to snooze on a train in West Virginia.

★

A St. Louis, Missouri law makes it a crime to drink beer from a bucket on any street curb.

★

It is illegal in Louisiana to shoot a bank teller with a water pistol while committing a bank robbery.

★

It is against the law to carry an ice cream cone in your pocket in Lexington, Kentucky.

★

In Richmond, Virginia it's illegal to flip a coin in a restaurant to see who pays for a coffee.

★

A law in Bexley, Ohio prohibits installing or using a slot machine in an outhouse.

★

North Carolina has a law against singing out of tune.

★

It is illegal to catch fish with your bare hands in Kansas.

LAWS, OLD & WEIRD

It is illegal to throw a bale of hay from a second floor window in Baltimore, Maryland.

★

A law in Corpus Christi, Texas forbids raising alligators in your home.

★

Frog-jumping contests within the city limits of Boston, Massachusetts, are against the law.

★

A New York City law prohibits having an unclothed mannequin in a store window.

★

In order for a pickle to be qualified as a pickle in the state of Connecticut, it must bounce.

★

Eating ice cream in public with a fork is strictly forbidden in Rosemead, California.

★

It's against New Jersey law for a man to knit during the fishing season.

★

Backed up by a $25 fine, it's against the law in South Bend, Indiana, for a monkey to smoke cigarettes.

★

Where else but in California would the law state that "lizards have the same rights as dogs."

PURE LAZINESS

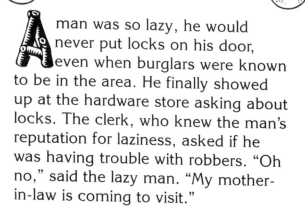

A man was so lazy, he would never put locks on his door, even when burglars were known to be in the area. He finally showed up at the hardware store asking about locks. The clerk, who knew the man's reputation for laziness, asked if he was having trouble with robbers. "Oh no," said the lazy man. "My mother-in-law is coming to visit."

One family was so lazy it took two of them to sneeze — one to throw his head back, and the other to say "ah-choo!"

"Doing nothing is a full-time job with never a day off."

PURE LAZINESS

Frustrated because his son would not lift a finger to help with chores around the farm, his father said, "When George Washington was your age, he already had a job as a surveyor." His son answered right back, "when George Washington was YOUR age, he was already President of the United States!"

༄

One farmer was so lazy he wouldn't carry in firewood if he was freezing to death. When it came time to build a new outhouse, he built it on the far side of the woodpile so his wife could carry in firewood on the way back from the outhouse!

༄

Lazy people are like blisters. They only show up after the work's all done.

༄

"He's so lazy he won't hit a lick at a snake."

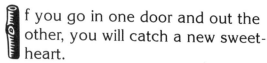
How to Catch a Sweetheart

If you go in one door and out the other, you will catch a new sweetheart.

🔊

If you encourage a stray dog, he will bring you a handsome sweetheart.

🔊

The first turtledove you hear in the spring will coo in the same direction as your new sweetheart. (Kentucky)

🔊

"For the first 3 weeks I dated this girl, I thought her name was 'un-uh.'"

🔊

If you build a good fire, your sweetheart loves you.

🔊

To tell your future love life, drink a mixture of mistletoe berries, honey and vinegar before going to bed. [Editor: mistletoe berries are poisonous!]

LOVE LORE

Gal Hunting

A country boy placed an ad in the local newspaper: WANTED — GOOD-LOOKING GAL FOR POSSIBLE MATRIMONY. MUST HAVE DEPENDABLE LATE-MODEL TRACTOR. SEND PHOTO OF TRACTOR.

YOU'LL BE AN OLD MAID IF YOU...

Look into a coffee pot.
Soak your bread or cake in a coffee cup.
Cut first into a cake of butter.
Wear a thimble on your left hand.
Sneeze three times in succession.
Plant a weeping willow tree.
Take the last biscuit on a plate.
Crook your little finger while holding
your cup.
Look under the bed. (Kentucky)

Love and Pickles

If a young man dreams he eats a pickle, he will marry a sour-tempered, older woman.

If a young girl dreams she eats a pickle, an old bachelor will kiss her.

If a boy eats a pickle, he is in love.

If a girl craves pickles, her love is returned. (Kentucky)

Love and Apples

Attach a piece of string to an apple and whirl it around before a fire. The girl whose apple falls off first will be the first to marry. The one whose apple stays on the string longest will never marry.

If you break an apple in two, you can get anyone you choose as your sweetheart.

If you can eat a crab apple without frowning, you can get any person you desire. (Kentucky)

Shoot up an apple seed. Your sweetheart lives in the direction it goes.

Peel an apple in one long strip and toss the peel backwards over your left shoulder. The shape the peel makes will show the initial of your future spouse.

Twist an apple stem while reciting the alphabet. The letter you are on when the stem comes out will tell the initial of your future husband or wife.

"A snuff box, watch, studs, sleeve-buttons, watch-chain, and one ring are all the jewelry a well-dressed man can wear." *The Gentlemen's Book of Etiquette and Manual on Politeness* by Cecil B. Hartley, 1860.

"Large hats make little women look like mushrooms." *Everyday Etiquette* by Marion Hartland and Virginia Van de Water, 1907.

"Do not leave children to their own devices near a lion's cage." *Good Manners For All Occasions* by Margaret E. Sangster, 1921

"Cavalry officers should never wear spurs in a ball-room." *Mixing in Society*, 1869

"Cast not thy bones under the table." *The Boke of Nurture, or Schoole of Good Manners*, compyled by Hugh Rodes, 1577. (sic)

MANNERS

George Washington was 15 years old when he copied the following rules of conduct from the 1640 translation of a 1595 French Jesuit book entitled *Rules of Civility and Decent Behavior*:

Put not off your Cloths in the presence of Others, nor go out of your Chamber half Drest.

Spit not in the Fire, nor Stoop low before it...

Kill no Vermin as Fleas, lice ticks etc in the Sight of Others.

In Speaking to men of Quality, do not lean nor Look them full in the Face, nor approach too near them [but] Keep a full Pace from them.

"Very little starch should be put in napkins. No one wishes to wipe a delicate lip on a board." *Manners and Social Uses*, Mrs. John Sherwood, 1897

19th century advice to the lady crossing a mud puddle: "Lift your skirt with one hand only. To use two hands is undignified."

> **"Never cackle or shriek."**
> *Etiquette for Americans, 1909*

MANNERS

"The woman who leaves a trail of perfume in her wake...ought to be set on a desert island."
Things That Are Not Done by Edgar and Diana Woods, 1937

"The person who snorts when she laughs is also out of order." *Manners for Millions* by Sephie C. Hadida, 1932

Proper young lady's behavior while walking down the street: "Never giggle; never walk with a wiggle." New York ca. 1845

"Without women, men would soon resume the savage state." *The American Code of Manners*, W.R. Andrews, 1880

MARK TWAIN'S WIT

Mark Twain was riding in a wagon when the driver ran over a big rock, and the humorist was unceremoniously jolted off. The driver came back and asked, "Are you hurt?" Twain replied, "No, but if I ever go to hell I would like to be taken there in your wagon, because I would be so glad to get there."

"Water taken in moderation cannot hurt anybody."

"Everybody is always talking about the weather, but nobody ever does anything about it."

"Let us live so that when we die, even the undertaker will be sorry."

"I have made it a rule not to smoke more than one cigar at the same time."

"Be good and you will be lonesome." (1897)

"All you need in this life is ignorance and confidence, and then success is sure."

"Clothes make the man. Naked people have little or no influence in society."

While discussing resolutions with several of the guests at a New Year's party, someone asked, "Are you making any resolutions this year, Mark?" "You bet," replied the writer. "I'm going to live within my income this year even if I have to borrow money to do it."

While relaxing on the deck of a Mississippi riverboat, a grubby roustabout approached the famous author and asked if he could shake his hand. "Pardon me if my mitt is a bit greasy, but I've just been cleaning a mess of catfish." "Pardon me too," said the humorist as he extended his hand toward the riverman. "I'm just getting over a touch of leprosy, myself."

"There is no use in walking five miles to fish when you can be just as unsuccessful near home."

"A use has been found for everything but snoring." May, 1892

"Cauliflower is nothing but cabbage with a college education."

"Man is the only animal that blushes, or needs to."

MARK TWAIN'S WIT

Returning home on the train after doing some out-of-season fishing, Mark Twain couldn't resist bragging to the gentleman sitting next to him about the twelve fish he had caught. Finally, the gentleman said to the author, "Do you know who I am?" Twain answered, "No, I don't." "I am the Game Warden." Twain in turn said, "You don't seem to know who I am." The Warden's answer was, "No, I don't." Said Twain, "I am the damnedest liar on earth." (1908)

"When angry, count to a hundred. When very angry, swear."

"Always do right. This will gratify some people, and astonish the rest."

"When I was a boy of 14, my father was so ignorant, I could hardly stand to have the old man around. But when I got to be 21, I was astonished at how much he had learned in seven years."

MARRIAGE

Two old maids were chatting over tea. "I advertised for a man in the paper last week," said the first. "You don't say!" said the second. "Did you get any replies?" "Oh yes, I received hundreds of them!" "Oh, that's good," said the first. "No, that's bad," said the second. "Why is it bad?" "Because all the replies were from women who said 'you can have mine!'"

Two ladies were talking when one turned to her friend and said, "I hear you have broken your engagement to John because your feelings toward him aren't the same. Are you going to return his ring?" "Oh no. My feelings toward the ring are the same as ever."

If you eat from a frying pan, it will rain on your wedding.

A girl who climbs in and out of a window will get a dumb husband.

Wedding Customs

"It is not the correct thing for enthusiastic friends to throw old shoes with such force as to break the carriage windows or frighten the horses." *The Correct Thing in Good Society* by Florence Howe Hall, 1902

Right after the marriage ceremony, the groom approached the preacher and asked him what he owed him. The preacher smiled and said, "Oh, pay me what you think this marriage is worth." The young man reached in his pocket and handed the preacher a dollar bill. The preacher thanked him and the young man continued to stand there, as if he were expecting something. After the awkward pause, the preacher asked, "Was there something else?" The groom said, "I was waiting for my change."

Do married people live longer than single people, or does it just SEEM longer?

No Hurry!

A farmer was standing in line at the post office when he turned around and saw the town doctor standing in line behind him. After chatting about the weather, the doctor asked how his wife was getting along. "Oh, she's not doing too good, Doc. A while back she fractured her jaw and she can't speak a word." "My goodness! I'll be out right away and take a look at her," said the doctor. "That's OK, Doc. Just come over sometime in the next three months or so when you're out in the area anyway."

MARRIAGE ADVICE

"Don't marry a man who has no time for dogs. Ten to one such a man will have only time for himself." *Things That Are Not Done* by Edgar and Diana Woods, 1937

"Don't woo a girl who keeps a diary."
The Cynic's Rules of Conduct by Chester Field, Jr., 1905

"If a woman has had more than four husbands, she poisons them — avoid her."
The American Chesterfield, early 1800s

Marriage Advice for Men

"Don't marry a woman who reads novels, and dreams of being a duchess, a countess, or the wife of a multimillionaire." *Don't for Everybody* by Frederic Reddale, 1907

If you make a bed neat, you'll marry a handsome man.

One husband at home is worth two in a saloon. *Clinton-Advo-cate Newspaper,* 1885

If you eat the last piece of food on a platter, you'll never marry.

If you splash water on your stomach when you wash dishes, you will marry a drunkard.

Lift your feet when you drive over a creek if you ever want to get married.

If you dream of fish, there will be a wedding.

If a woman gets two forks on her plate, she will have two husbands. (Kentucky)

Marry in brown, you'll live in town.
Marry in red, better be dead.
Marry in green, shame to be seen.
Marry in yellow, you're ashamed of your fellow.
Marry in blue, always prove true.
Marry in black, you'll wish yourself back.
Marry in white, you've chosen all right. (Virginia)

A man goes to a skin doctor with a rare skin disease. The doctor says, "Try a milk bath." So the guy goes to the grocery store and tells the dairy manager he needs enough milk to take a bath. The dairy guys ask, "You want that past-eur-ized?" "Nah," the man replied. "Up to my chin should do it."

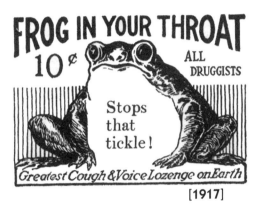

FROG IN YOUR THROAT
10 ¢

ALL DRUGGISTS

Stops that tickle!

Greatest Cough & Voice Lozenge on Earth

[1917]

A carnival barker vigorously pounded his chest and said, "Ladies and gentlemen, look what this wonderful snake oil has done for me. Note my marvelous constitution, perfect teeth and healthy skin. Would you possibly guess that I am over 200 years old?"

A farmer sitting in the front row looked rather skeptical, and leaned over and asked the barker's assistant, "Is he really that old?" "You can't prove it by me," said the assistant. "I've only been working for him for 120 years."

While motoring down a backwoods road, a country doctor came upon a man trying to get his stubborn mule to go. "What seems to be the trouble?" asked the doctor. The frustrated man told him that he needed to get to town but when his mule took a balky spell like this, not heaven nor hell could make him move.

The doctor quickly opened his black bag and took out a bottle that contained a nasty-looking brown liquid and rubbed some on the mule's flank. The animal pawed the ground, bowed his neck, rolled his eyes, and then went pitching and snorting across the prairie. The man then turned to the doctor and said, "Doc! hurry and rub some of that stuff on me so I can catch up with him!"

Soothe earaches with the juice of fresh mistletoe.

A man took his wife to the doctor who put a thermometer in her mouth and told her to keep her mouth shut for three minutes. When they were leaving, the husband pulled the doctor aside and asked, "What will you take for that thing, Doc?"

MEDICINE

I n 1900, you could buy marijuana, heroin, and morphine over the counter at corner drugstores. One pharmacist announced, "Heroin clears the complexion, gives buoyancy to the mind, regulates the stomach and the bowels, and is a perfect guardian of health."

A gullible buyer paid $20,000 in gold at an auction for a sealed book entitled, *The Onliest and Deepest Secrets of the Medical Art*. It was written by Dutch physician and chemist Hermann Boerhaave, who died in 1738. The buyer was shocked to discover when he opened the sealed book that the pages were entirely blank except for a handwritten note penned by the author that read: "Keep your head cool, your feet warm, and you'll make the best doctor poor."

In the 1830s, ketchup was sold in drug stores as a patent medicine.

Rattlesnake venom was used to cure epilepsy in the early 20th century.

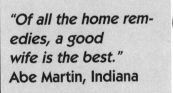
"Of all the home remedies, a good wife is the best."
Abe Martin, Indiana

Moses Jones made the best moonshine in the whole county. The revenuers finally caught him in the act of making moonshine and brought him before the judge. The judge was in a good mood, so he asked, "Are you the Moses who can make the sun dark?" Moses looked up at the judge, "No, your honor. I'm the Moses who can make the moonshine."

Two moonshiners were trying to cheer up their old friend Ben, who was on his deathbed. "Ben, is there anything we can do for you after you're gone?" In a quivering voice, Ben told them, "I've been holding back a quart of my best moonshine, and boys, I'd be grateful if you'd pour it over my grave when I'm gone." The two moonshiners looked sheepishly at one another and after a moment of reflection one of them finally said, "We'd be glad to do that for you, old Pard, but if you don't care, we'll strain it through our kidneys first."

If you're rich and you drink, you're an alcoholic.
But if you're poor and you drink, you're a DRUNK!

After his plumbing was hopelessly backed up, a home owner in Fairbanks, Alaska, called in plumber after plumber, but none could find the source of the problem.

In desperation, one final plumber was called in, and he correctly diagnosed the problem: there was one dead moose in the septic tank. Apparently, the moose had fallen into the tank and drowned. After they fished it out, the plumbing returned to normal.

A saloon owner in Fairbanks, Alaska, once had a pet moose who routinely got drunk and staggered around the town. In an effort to prevent this, lawmakers passed an ordinance making it a crime for a moose to walk on the sidewalk, thus legally preventing him from entering the saloon. A law was also passed making it a crime to get a moose drunk!

The Mosquito Wager

While prospecting for gold near the mosquito-infested Big Blue River in 1849, two miners made a wager. They put up stakes to see which of them could withstand the punishing bites of swarms of mosquitos the longest. They stripped off all their clothes, sat close to each other on the banks of the river, and waited for the attack to begin. Their only protection was that each would smoke a cigar.

When swarm after swarm of hungry mosquitos attacked them, one of the men decided to call it quits and dived in the river to escape the swarms of mosquitos. As he stood up, the business end of the other man's cigar accidentally touched his hindquarters. He immediately jumped up and shouted, "The great-granddaddy of the whole flock just stabbed me!"

A man in Maryland claimed that mosquitos had completely drained all his blood. He eventually had to start writing them IOUs. After he moved away, the mosquitos sent him greeting cards every father's day because they had so much of his blood that he was considered kin!

MOSQUITO TALES

Two mosquitoes were buzzing around the head of a drunken man when they finally landed on his arm. One of the mosquitos turned to the other and said, "You bite him. I'm driving."

As a teenager living in Mexico in the summer of 1963, I learned from my Mexican host family that a sure cure for the itch of a mosquito bite was to rub it with a lime. One time my roommate and I bought a bottle of Tequila. We knew the local custom was to drink it with lime and salt, so late one night we snuck into the kitchen and pilfered some salt and a lime. Jose, our host, must have seen us leave the kitchen with the lime, and figured we were having mosquito problems in our room. Just as we secretly began imbibing the tequila, we heard a loud knock on the door and in burst Jose, who began spraying for mosquitos. Apparently, the poisonous cloud of the insecticide obscured his view of the tequila, because if he saw it, he didn't let on.

A mosquito flaps its wings 600 times a second.

The mosquito is the world's most indestructible insect. It can survive in habitats ranging from the frozen North Pole to the jungles of the Equator.

129

MULE EGGS

In the days before tractors, a good mule was prized by any farmer worth his salt. One time, two city slickers from Chicago hit upon a money-making scheme. They took the train down to the Ozarks where mules were cheap and plentiful. Their plan was to buy mules for practically nothing, and ship them up North where Illinois farmers would pay a pretty penny for them.

After the Chicago men arrived by train, they started making inquiries about who had mules to sell. The local farmers got wind of their motives, and let it be known that they were not selling any mules, period.

Giving up in disgust, the Chicago men were preparing to leave when they were approached by an enterprising farmer. He explained that he didn't have any full grown mules to sell, but he would be glad to sell mule eggs to them, which would soon hatch out to be valuable farm animals. The city slickers agreed to buy two dozen mule eggs at $50 each, and the farmer promised to return the next day with the eggs.

The excited farmer then painted two dozen watermelons with silver paint and brought them back the next day in a wagon. After carefully counting his money, he left the eggs on the depot platform and hastily departed.

As the businessmen were loading the mule eggs on the train, one of them dropped an egg, which proceeded to roll down the hill. When it got to the bottom, it smashed into a big rock and split open. The impact frightened a jack rabbit that was hiding next to the rock, and it took off running. Of course, the city slickers thought the rabbit had jumped out of the mule egg. One of them looked at the other and shrugged, "it looks like we bought the wrong kind of eggs. *These mules run too fast to plow!*"

Mule Superstitions

When mules kick their stalls or bray more frequently than usual, bad weather is coming.

To tame a mule, bite it on the ear.

Seeing a white mule is an omen of good fortune.

The Long-Eared Mule

A farmer bought a new mule that had especially long ears. He told the two country boys who worked for him to unload the mule and put him in the barn. Right off, they could see that the mule's ears were too long to fit in the barn. After putting their heads together, they decided to saw the overhead of the barn out so the mule could walk right in the barn.

As they began sawing out the overhead the farmer walked up and asked why they were sawing out the top of the barn. When they told him the mule's ears were too long to go into the barn, the farmer said, "Why don't you just get a shovel and dig the dirt out of the ground below, so the mule can walk on in?"

The two country boys looked at each other and said, "Boss, it's his ears that are too long, not his feet!

It's against the law to wash a mule on the sidewalk in Cullpeper, VA.

The Fastest Mule Alive

When he heard his neighbor wanted to buy a mule, a farmer took his sorry old mule down to his neighbor's place. After shaking howdy, the neighbor asked, "Is he fast?" "Fast?" asked the farmer. "The last time I rode him I gave him one little kick with the heel of my boot, and he nearly bucked me off. Then he tore down a row of fence posts, galloped through a week's laundry, ran right through the side of the barn, tore across the garden patch, knocking down all the corn and vanished into the woods." On hearing that, the neighbor just shook his head and said, "That mule must be blind." "Oh, he's not blind," the farmer said. "He just don't give a damn!"

Mule Meter

If tail is wet - rain
If tail is swinging - wind
If tail is frozen - cold
If tail is gone - cyclone

"A mule in a tuxedo is still a mule."

How to Sell a Dead Mule

A man who recently moved from the city bought a new tractor and was out plowing his field when his tractor got stuck in mud. A local farmer who was driving by stopped his truck and walked to the fence. He called over to the city fellow, "What you need is a good mule." "Where can I buy one?" asked the city man. "Well, it just so happens that I have one for sale for one hundred dollars. The city man said, "I'll take him." The farmer wanted cash on the barrel head, so the city man counted out one hundred dollars in cash, and the farmer agreed to bring out the mule the next day.

The following afternoon a truck pulled up and the farmer got out. Shaking his head, he said, "I'm sorry, but I've got bad news. I went out after breakfast and the mule was dead." The city man asked for his money back but the farmer said, "I wish I could give you your money back, but I've already spent it." Not wanting to start a fight, the city man said, "Well, unload the mule anyway." Surprised, the farmer asked, "What are you going to do with a dead mule?" "I'm going to raffle him off," said the city man. The farmer shrugged, but unloaded the dead mule.

About a month later, the farmer and the city man ran into each other at the barber shop. "What did you ever do with that dead mule?" asked the farmer. "Just like I said, I raffled him off. I sold one hundred tickets at two dollars each and made a hundred dollars profit." "Didn't anyone complain?" asked the farmer. "Just one guy, so I gave him his two dollars back!"

MIKE NOLAN

HIS MULE & HIS CART.

The Lost Mule

After searching for a week for a lost mule, the owner offered a country boy two bits if he could find him. In about an hour the country boy came back leading the mule. "How did you find him so quick?" asked the owner. "I just thought where I'd go if I were a mule. I went there and there he was!"

Uncle Semour

One old lady was upset about the size of the mosquitos that swarmed around her house. She complained that, "The young mosquitos eat my chickens, ducks and turkeys. The older ones devour my goats, pigs, and even my bull!"

One time she claimed they were particularly hungry and set their sites on her prized mule, Uncle Semour. One of the big mosquitos swallowed Uncle Semour and attempted to fly away with him. Before the mosquito could get much altitude, Semour let go with both hind legs and broke the mosquito's neck.

A mule named Boston Curtis was elected Republican precinct committee-man from Milton, Washington in 1938.

Photo by Wayne Erbsen

"When you go to a mule's house, don't talk about ears."

~Jamaican proverb

MY OWN GRANDPA!

"I married a widow with a grown daughter. My father fell in love with my stepdaughter and married her, thus becoming my son-in-law. So, my stepdaughter became my mother because she was my father's wife."

"My father's wife gave birth to a son. He was, of course, my father's brother-in-law and also my uncle, for he was the brother of my stepmother."

"Accordingly, my wife was my grandmother, because she was my father's mother. I was my wife's husband and grandchild at the same time. And, since the husband of a person's grandmother is his grandfather, I am my own grandpa."

"You can tame a mule but a doggone fool is a fool until he dies."
~Uncle Dave Macon

Some of the stranger names found on birth certificates include: Ammonia, Aspirin, Autopsy, Constipation, Depression, Diaphragm, Distemper, Esophagus, Eczema, Halitosis, Hang Nails, Iodine, Latrina, Listerine, Morphine, Nausea, Vaseline.

My all-time favorite name is Nosmo King. It seems that an "expectant" father was nervously pacing in the waiting room of the delivery ward. When the happy news came that he was the father of a son, the man was suddenly at a loss to tell the nurse what to name his newborn son. Just then, he looked up and saw the "No Smoking" sign, and in his haste he said, "We'll call him "Nosmo King.""

Weird Place Names

Blue Balls, Pennsylvania and Ohio
Cut n' Shoot, Texas
Gnaw Bone, Indiana
Hell, Michigan
Hooker, Oklahoma
Hogshooter, Oklahoma
Intercourse, Alabama
Knock 'em Stiff, Ohio
Loafer's Glory, North Carolina
Slap-Out, Alabama
Rabbit Hash, Kentucky
Toad Suck, Arkansas
What Cheer, Iowa

If Your Nose Itches...

There's a hole in your britches.

Someone is thinking about you.

You'll quarrel with a loved one.

You'll kiss a fool.

If the right side of your nose itches, a woman will come to visit.

If the left side of your nose itches, a man will come to visit.

If the end of your nose itches, a person riding in a buggy will visit you.

If your nose tickles, you will kiss an old person before the day's out.

It's impossible to sneeze with your eyes open.

A Sneeze on...

Monday is for danger
Tuesday, you kiss a stranger
Wednesday, you get a letter
Thursday, you get something better
Friday is for sorrow
Saturday, you see your sweetheart
   tomorrow

The Biggest Change

An Old West lawman was asked at his 100th birthday, "What was the biggest change that happened when everybody starting driving cars?" The old man thought for a minute and finally replied, "We didn't hang as many horse thieves as we used to."

The Upper or the Lower

After visiting the dentist, a senior citizen went to the Department of Motor Vehicles and waited in line to get a new tag for his car. When his turn came, the old gentleman filled out all the paperwork and the clerk handed him his new tag, saying, "Here's your new plate, Sir." The old geezer looked at the tag for a second and then asked, "Is this the upper or the lower plate?"

Only Three Choices

Two old guys were sitting on a bench in front of a hardware store. One of them turned to the other and said, "You know, my wife has been complaining about the way I wear my hair." The second man laughed and said, "Tell her there's only three choices: parted, unparted and departed."

OLD AGE

They held a fiddler's convention at the Moose Lodge and among the contestants was an old-timer who was close to ninety years of age. Entering the senior division, he handily won first place and walked away with a  trophy and a crisp one hundred dollar bill. A reporter from the local paper asked him, "Pardon me Sir, but how do you manage to play so well at your advanced age?" The old man thought for a moment and replied, "If I can manage to  remember the whole tune, I know I have a darn good chance to win!"

Asking an old lady her age is like asking a used car salesman if the odometer is correct. You know that both of them have been set back, but you don't know how far!

n old-timer who was nearly deaf had the reputation of being rather stingy. One time another old geezer asked him about the strange looking wire tied around his ear. "Is that some kind of a new-fangled hearing aid?" his friend asked. "Nope," he answered. "It's just a plain old wire." "Well, how in the heck does that help you hear better?" asked his friend. The stingy old man answered back, "When people see that wire, they talk louder."

An elderly couple was having memory problems. One time the husband got off the couch and asked his wife if she'd like some ice-cream. "Yes," she replied, "I'd like vanilla, but you better write it down so you don't forget." "I won't forget," said her husband. "And I'd like some of that chocolate sauce over it too. You better write it down so you don't forget." "I won't forget," he reassured her.

In about fifteen minutes, the husband returned with two plates of scrambled eggs. The wife looked at the eggs and said, "I told you to write it down. I said I wanted toast with my eggs!"

he Pony Express was only in operation from April 1860 to November 1861.

★ Jesse James was called "Dingus" by his friends.

★ Lieutenant Colonel George Armstrong Custer graduated last in his class at West Point.

★ Barbed wire was first used to fence cattle in 1874.

★ Bat Masterson, famed lawman of Dodge City, Kansas, became sports editor of the New York Morning Telegraph. He died in 1921 at his desk at the age of 68 of natural causes.

★ Wyatt Earp kicked the bucket at the ripe old age of 79 in Los Angeles, California in 1929.

Photo by Wayne Erbsen

★ The crack of a bull-whip is the sound it makes when it breaks the sound barrier.

It took Crazy Bob Womack nearly twelve years, but in 1890, he had a major gold strike near Cripple Creek, Colorado. Although the mine would eventually bring in over three million dollars worth of gold, Crazy Bob got drunk one night and sold it for $300. When he died in 1909, he was broke.

Photo by Wayne Erbsen

Kit Carson

When famed scout Kit Carson was a lad of fourteen, he was apprenticed to a saddle-maker in Franklin, Missouri. In 1826, he ran away, and a reward of one cent was reportedly offered for his return.

Old West Wisdom
Never try to influence a man against his inclination when he is hungry.

THE OLD WEST

Black Bart, P O 8

Though most Old West outlaws were not known for writing poetry, one exception was the legendary Black Bart. In the 1870s, he held up twenty-eight stage coaches in California's gold country and always left a poem as his calling card.

> *I've labored long and hard for bread*
> *For honor and for riches*
> *But on my corns too long you've tread*
> *You fine haired sons of bitches.*
>   **~Black Bart, the P O 8**

The famed gunfight at the OK Corral took place on Fremont Street in Tombstone, Arizona Territory on October 26, 1881. By most accounts, it lasted less than one minute.

Until smokeless gunpowder was invented in 1895, the air at most shootouts in the Old West was so filled with smoke that it's a wonder that anybody got shot at all.

Cowboy Insult
His family tree is a shrub.

THE OLD WEST

The first big train robbery was committed by Sam Bass and his five companions in August or September of 1877. They gleefully hauled off 3,000 freshly-minted twenty-dollar gold pieces.

Sam Bass was well-loved in Texas for his kindness and generosity. After robbing passengers on a train, he always left each passenger with a dollar so they could afford to buy breakfast.

It was 1914 when the automobile was first used to commit a bank robbery. The crime was committed by Henry Starr, the nephew of Belle Starr. During a later bank robbery, Starr's car broke down and he was killed by Sheriff's deputies. In all, Starr held up fifty banks.

Clay Allison, one of the most feared outlaws of the Old West, once raced and war-whooped his horse through town wearing only his boots! On his tombstone, are written these words:

**HE NEVER KILLED A MAN
WHO DIDN'T NEED KILLING.**

Brags & Boasts

He'd charge hell with a bucket of water.

He'd fight a rattlesnake and give it the first bite.

He could spit in a wildcat's eye.

He told lies so well a man would have to be a fool not to believe them.

"I'll kick yo' pants up 'round yo' neck so tight, it'll choke you to death."

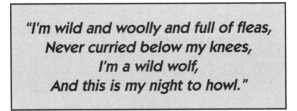

> *"I'm wild and woolly and full of fleas,*
> *Never curried below my knees,*
> *I'm a wild wolf,*
> *And this is my night to howl."*

Jim Bollman Collection

147

THE OLD WEST

Buffalo Turd Pie

Cowboys had an unspoken rule that they all obeyed: complain about the cooking and you're the new cook. One time this old cow puncher got fed up with the lousy cooking he had to endure. He threw down his fork and said, "I CAN'T EAT ANOTHER BITE OF THIS SLOP!"

Knowing he was the new cook, the cowpuncher devised a cruel plan. He hitched up the wagon and rode out on the prairie 'til he came to a nice collection of buffalo turds. He carefully selected one large turd, wrapped it in a piece of burlap, and loaded it on the wagon. When he got back to the bunkhouse, he carried his secret prize into the kitchen. There he rolled out a pie shell, added the bufalo turd, and cooked up the finest buffalo turd pie man had ever known.

After supper, the old cowboy brought out his pie to the "oos and aahs" of the smiling cowboys. He served the first piece to the former cook, who quickly grabbed his fork and took a great big bite of that buffalo turd pie. His eyes started to water, his face turned pale, and through clenched teeth he said, "THIS TASTES LIKE BUFFALO TURD PIE! It's good though."

Last Words

"Every man for his principles. Hurrah for Jeff Davis. Let 'er go, men!" Boone Helm, hanged in Virginia City.

"Can't you hurry this up a bit? I hear they eat dinner in Hades at twelve sharp. I don't aim to be late." Black Jack Ketchum, hanged in Clayton, New Mexico.

"I wish there was time for just one more bowl of chili." Kit Carson

OLD WEST WOMEN

nnie Oakley's real name was Phoebe Moses, but they all called her "Little Sure Shot." A poor back-country orphan girl, she could handle a gun by the age of twelve better than anyone before or since. At the invita- tion of Kaiser Wilhelm II of Ger-

many, she shot the ashes off a ciga- rette he was holding in his mouth.

In 1883, Belle Starr became the first female tried for a major crime by the "Hanging Judge," the Honorable Isaac C. Parker. She was charged and convicted as a horse thief and sen- tenced to six months in jail.

The only woman known to have led a cattle drive was Margaret Heffernan Borland (1824-1873). In the spring of 1873, she left her home in Victoria, Texas, with 2,500 cattle. She was accompanied by her two sons who were under fifteen years of age, her seven-year-old daughter, an even younger granddaughter, plus a num- ber of trail hands. She managed to lead the entire party to Wichita, Kan- sas but died shortly after, presumably from an illness known as "trail fever."

ONE HUNDRED YEARS AGO

☞ The average American worker earned 22 cents/hour.

☞ Coca Cola contained cocaine instead of caffeine.

☞ The average life expectancy in the United States was forty-seven.

☞ Only 14 percent of the homes in the United States had a bathtub.

☞ There were only 8,000 cars and 144 miles of paved roads in the US.

☞ The maximum speed limit in most cities was ten mph.

☞ Only eight percent of the homes had a telephone. A three minute call from Denver to New York City cost eleven dollars.

☞ Alabama, Mississippi, Iowa and Tennessee were each more heavily populated than California.

☞ More than 95 percent of all births in the US took place at home.

☞ Most women only washed their hair once a month and used borax or egg yolks for shampoo.

☞ Not yet discovered was Plutonium, insulin, and antibiotics, Scotch tape, crossword puzzles, canned beer or iced tea.

☞ There was no Mother's Day or Father's Day.

OUTHOUSE TALES

An old man got up in the middle of the night to go to the outhouse, but no one had remembered to tell him that they had moved the outhouse that afternoon. He walked to the place where the outhouse had always stood and helplessly looked around for it in the total darkness. Thinking he must be sleepwalking, he started back to bed but before he knew it, he fell right down in the old outhouse hole!

Hopelessly trapped down in the hole, the old man started yelling. He screamed, "Fire! Fire!" Everyone came running, and soon they had him out of the hole and half-way cleaned up. His son asked him, "Pop, I just gotta ask you why you yelled "fire?" The old man looked at him sheepishly and replied, "I knew no one would come running if I yelled, "Feces! Feces!"

Photo by Wayne Erbsen

OUTHOUSE TALES

The grand prize for the most expensive outhouse in history must surely go to the Delaware Water Gap National Recreation Area in northeastern Pennsylvania. In 1998, they built an outhouse which cost $784,014. It didin't even have running water! And all this when the Park Service was not exactly flush.

> *"Henry...I'm sorry to hear your bathroom caught fire and burned last night. " "Yeah," replied Henry, "It was a great loss. I'm just glad the flames didn't touch the house."*

A country woman wanted a new-fangled bathroom built on her house, so she went to the bank to borrow money. Never having been to a bank before, she was plenty nervous. The receptionist escorted her into the office of the bank president, who smiled and asked her how he could be of service. She sat down on the edge of her chair and blurted right out, "I want to borrow money so I can put a bathroom in my house."

The president replied cautiously, "I don't believe you have an account with us. Where have you done your business before?" Without hesitating she replied, "Oh, out back in the bushes."

OUTHOUSE TALES

Who's Crazy?

While at the county fair, a farmer paid a visit to the outhouse. Once inside the two-holer, he saw a nervous-looking man dropping a twenty dollar gold piece down in the outhouse hole. The man was taking off his coat in preparation to climb down in the hole when the farmer said, "What on earth are you doing climbing down there? Are you crazy?" "No, I'm not crazy," replied the man. "I just dropped my grandfather's gold watch down in the hole. And if you think I'm going down there just for that old watch, then you're the one that's crazy!"

The Perfect Gift

If you're one of those people who craves their own outhouse but are not handy with a hammer and a saw, there's a company in Arkansas that has outhouse kits available! Everything is included except a copy of *The Outhouse Papers!*
www.cowboycooking.com

Fart Proverb
"A farting horse will never tire,
And a farting man
Is the man to hire."

PAIN & SUFFERING

A country fellow went to town to see the doctor. The doctor asked him, "What seems to be the trouble?" "I hurt all over," replied the man. "Everywhere I touch, it hurts." The man touched his elbow, and he winced in pain. "See what I mean, Doc?" "OK," said the doctor, "touch your head." "Ouch!" yelped the man. "Your knee." Again the man cried out in pain.

The doctor scratched his chin and then ordered a full set of x-rays. The doctor then told him to come back in three days. When the man returned the doctor said, "I've found your problem." "Great Doc, what is it?"

"You've broken your finger."

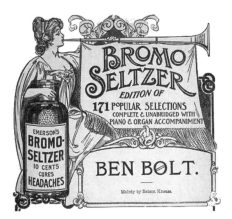

Outhouse Quiz
Which state has the most outhouses?
Alaska

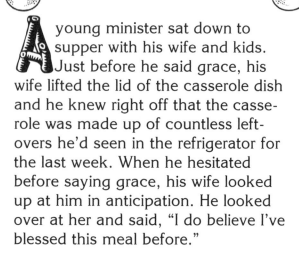

PREACHER TALES

A young minister sat down to supper with his wife and kids. Just before he said grace, his wife lifted the lid of the casserole dish and he knew right off that the casserole was made up of countless leftovers he'd seen in the refrigerator for the last week. When he hesitated before saying grace, his wife looked up at him in anticipation. He looked over at her and said, "I do believe I've blessed this meal before."

> *"When I see a man preach I like to see him act as if he were fighting bees."* ~Abraham Lincoln

A preacher met a country boy on the streets of a small town. After chatting for a few minutes, the preacher asked, "Do you want to go to Heaven?" The country boy looked startled and answered, "Well Sir, no I don't." The preacher was aghast and said, "Now young man, you must think about this carefully. Don't you want to go to Heaven?" The country boy again said he didn't want to go. In desperation, the preacher finally said, "When you die, don't you want to go to Heaven?" The country boy brightened up and replied, "Oh, you mean when I die? I thought you meant I'd be goin' right now."

PREACHER TALES

The Preacher & the Bear

Disheartened over low church attendance, one Sunday the preacher decided to go hunting instead. He got out in the woods and was tromping around when he met face to face with a huge grizzly bear. In his haste to shoot, the preacher fumbled and dropped his gun. The bear then grabbed him and was about to devour him when the preacher made a silent prayer, "Oh Lord, please forgive me for missing services today and please grant me this one wish. Make this bear a Christian." The next instant the bear relaxed his grip and the preacher dropped to his knees. The bear then folded his paws together and began to pray out loud, "Dear Lord, bless this food I am about to receive..."

Library of Congress

"He was so slick, he could charm the preacher's wife out of her corset."

PREACHER TALES

An old country preacher who had always sermonized against the evils of alcohol, took sick and it looked like the end was near. His wife asked the doctor if there was anything he could take to ease his pain. The doctor wrinkled his brow and suggested, "A shot of whiskey each day might make him more comfortable." "But doctor," she protested, "He's never even tasted alcohol before. How am I going to get him to take it?" The doctor suggested, "Slip the whiskey into his milk. He might drink it then."

The preacher lingered for almost a week, and even seemed to perk up when his wife offered him his daily glass of milk which was secretly laced with whiskey. When the end finally came near, the preacher motioned to his wife to come close so he could whisper his last words before he died.

As his wife knelt close to his bedside, the preacher said, "Whatever you do, *don't sell that cow!*"

PREACHER TALES

All the Hay

One Sunday morning a country boy decided to go to church. He walked in the door and he was shocked to find the church was completely empty. When he saw the preacher, he asked, "Have I got the wrong day?" "No, this is the right day," the preacher assured him. "There's just not been many people coming to church lately. Shall we go ahead with the service?" asked the preacher. The country boy answered, "Well, if I went to feed my cattle and only one showed up, I'd sure feed him."

So the preacher launched into his full sermon and before he knew it, two and a  half hours had gone by. As the country boy was leaving, the preacher asked him how he liked the sermon. "Well, Sir, if I went to feed my cattle and only one showed up, I sure wouldn't feed him all the hay!"

> *"The more fuss a man makes when he gets religion, the less likely it is to stick." (1909)*

Food

Bacon	.12/lb
Butter	.18/lb
Chicken	.07/lb
Coffee	.15/lb
Eggs	.12dz
Lemons	.15/dz
Loaf of bread	.05
Sugar	.04/lb

Men's Clothes

Linen collar	.25
Pants	1.25
Shirt	.50
Shoes	1.25
Suspenders	.25

Ladies Clothes

Skirt	4.00
Blouse	.35
Corset	.40
Shawl	.50
Shoes	1.50
Silk petticoat	5.00

Miscellaneous

Brass bed	3.00
Shave & a haircut	.25
Sofa	9.98
Cadillac	750.00

The Klondike in 1898

Butter	3.00/lb
Eggs	3.00/dz
Gallon of milk	16.00
Onions	1.50/ea

RAILROAD TRIVIA

Cornelius Vanderbilt was the wealthiest railroad tycoon in America. When he slept, he had the legs of his bed placed in dishes of salt to ward off evil spirits. He once fired a man who worked for him because he didn't like his name, Spittles. As a young man, Vanderbilt was in the first major train wreck in America on November 8, 1833. After that, it took nearly thirty years for him to overcome his fear of travel by rail. Also injured in the same wreck was John Quincy Adams.

In 1859, German inventor Frederick Albrect attached large helium-filled balloons to the railroad cars to help climb mountains.

Luther Burbank frequently "summoned" his sister telepathically to board the next train to visit their ailing mother.

The first man to be run over by a train was William Huskisson. He is honored by a statue in Pimlico Gardens, London.

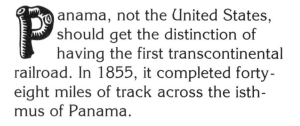

RAILROAD TRIVIA

Panama, not the United States, should get the distinction of having the first transcontinental railroad. In 1855, it completed forty-eight miles of track across the isthmus of Panama.

———•———

To calculate the speed of a train, count the number of rail-clicks you hear in 26.6 seconds. This will tell you the speed of the train in miles per hour.

———•———

Of all the railroad inventions, this one takes the cake! In 1895, Henry Latimer Simmons of Wickes, Montana received a patent that allowed two railroad cars to pass each other on a single track. Each car was equipped with tracks on the sloping roof of its cars.

———•———

Forget about taking the train in Afghanistan or Somalia. Not an inch of track has ever been laid in either country.

———•———

Railroad Superstition
Make a wish on seeing a freight train. Count the cars "yes, no, maybe so" to see if your wish will come true.

RAILROADS

Two bums were sleeping near the railroad track when a train came along and ran over the LEFT side of one of them. He was rushed to the hospital where the doctor announced, "He's all RIGHT now!"

A California inventor by the name of I.M.S.R. Mathewson came up with a street car with the motor disguised inside the head of a fake horse to keep real horses from being frightened.

Photo by Wayne Erbsen

Two women on a train were arguing about a window, and they called the porter to mediate. "If this window is open," one declared, "I shall catch cold and will surely die." The other woman solemnly announced, "If the window is shut, I will suffocate and die." The two glared at each other as the helpless porter tried to think of a solution. Finally, a drunk sitting nearby said, "First, open the window. That will kill the first one. Then shut it, which will kill the second one. Then we can have some peace!"

RAILROAD SLANG

Banjo: fireman's shovel
Bull: railroad policeman
Crowbar hotel: jail
Crummy: caboose
Egg: railroad policeman
Flip: to board a moving train
Fresh fish: a new hand
Gafer: section boss
Gandy dance: section worker
Gasket: doughnut
Grease the pig: oil the engine
Gum shoe: railroad detective
Hasher: waitress
Hogger: engineer
Hotshot: a fast train
Jailhouse spuds: waffled potatoes
Jerkwater: small town
Kettle: small locomotive
Lizard scorcher: a cook
Mud chicken: a surveyor
Mule: brakeman
Parlor boy: flagman
Pearl diver: dishwasher
Rat: a freight car
Rattler: a fast freight train
Red eye: stop signal
Redball: a fast freight train
Reefer: refrigerator car
Roughneck: a brakeman
Shiny pants: a railway clerk
Silk hat: a railway official
Sinker: doughnut
Toothpick: a railroad tie
Torpedoes: beans
Ukulele: a short-handled shovel
Whiskers: seniority

Students in a rural school were asked by their teacher to identify various animals. She held up a picture of a deer and called on one small boy to identify it. The boy was tongue-tied and couldn't think of the word. To give him a hint, the teacher said, "It's the same word that your mother calls your father." The boy brightened up and said, "Oh, I know. It's a jerk!"

THE SCHOOLMASTER

Either Way

Members of a school board were interviewing a new teacher for a rural school. One conservative member asked him if he believed in evolution. The teacher didn't bat an eye. "I don't know how you feel about it, but I can teach it either way."

Little George came home from school and asked his dad for some help with his arithmetic. "My teacher wants me to find the least common denominator." "Goodness gracious!" said his dad. "Haven't they found that thing yet? They were looking for it back when I was a kid."

Teacher: "Who can name five things that contain milk?"
Johnny: "Butter, cheese, ice cream, two cows."

A student told his father he had gotten an A on an algebra test. "That's

good, son. Say something in algebra." The son replied, "Pie-R Square." "Now son, I don't know much about algebra, but I know that pies are round. Cornbread is square.

What has four legs, long ears, sleeps standing up, lives in a stable or barn and can see equally well from either end?

(A Blind Mule)

SCHOOL DAZE

A teacher called on one little country boy and asked, "Johnny, what month has twenty-eight days in it?" The boy was stumped. While he was desperately trying to remember the answer, his classmates started to giggle. The teacher hushed the other students and patiently repeated her question, "Johnny, tell me what month has twenty-eight days in it?" Right then, little Johnny stood up and shouted, "All of them!"

— THE SPELLIN' CLASS —

"I have never let my schooling inter-fere with my education." ~Mark Twain

Benny and Bobby Joe had always been the best of friends. One fall day they hiked way back in the mountains digging ginseng, or "sang," as they called it. Benny was sliding down a big rock when a copperhead rattlesnake reached up and bit him on his backside. Grabbing his buttocks, Benny yelled, "I've been snake bit on my rear! Run and get Doc Hopkins and bring him up here quick!"

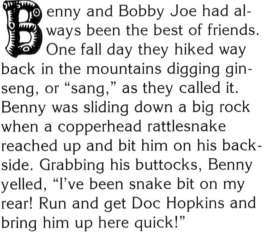

So Bobby Joe ran down the mountain and breathlessly burst into the doctor's office. The Doc said he had too many patients to tend to but told Bobby Joe exactly what to do. "Take your knife and lance the bite and then suck out all the poison. Then bring him into the office."

When Bobby Joe finally got back up the mountain to Benny, he told his friend, "I've got good news and bad news. Which do you want first?" Benny hesitated and then said, "Gimme the good news first." "OK," said Bobby Joe, "I found the doctor's office, and he was there." Getting agitated, Benny cried out, "Well, what did he say?" "Well, that's the bad news," said Bobby Joe. "He said you're gonna die!"

STRANGE HAPPENINGS

A man was asked to submit a urine sample before being sentenced for stealing Christmas presents off doorsteps in August of 1998. The sample he produced was curiously cold but was tested anyway. The test came back positive for pregnancy. He was tested a second time, and this sample (warm) tested positive for cocaine. Investigators aren't certain whose urine he first gave them, but his wife, who accompanied him to the testing, was pregnant. Although the man was eligible to receive only probation for the charge of stealing, the switched-urine trick got him a year in prison.

As a publicity stunt, daredevil Bobby Leech rode a barrel over Niagara Falls. He survived, but nearly broke every bone in his body. After he recovered, he went on a world  tour. However, while he was in New Zealand in 1911, he slipped on a banana peel and later died.

Luck in a Bottle

Flat broke and without prospects for a job, a man was walking along a San Francisco beach in 1949, when he found a bottle that had washed up on the shore. Examining it, he found a note inside the bottle that read:

> *"To avoid confusion, I leave my entire estate to the lucky person who finds this bottle and to my attorney, share and share alike. Daisy Alexander, June 20, 1937."*

The man soon discovered that the note was a genuine will from the former Daisy Singer of the Singer Sewing Machine Co. Her will left a fortune of 12 million dollars to the finder of the note in the bottle.

No one knows why Daisy Alexander wrote her simple will, corked it in a bottle, and threw it into the Thames River in London. From there it floated down the Thames, across the North Sea, to Scandinavia, Russia, Siberia, through the Bering Straits and into the Pacific Ocean, where it drifted for some twelve years until it washed ashore at San Francisco. In the final settlement, the man received 6 million dollars plus $80,000 a year from Singer stock.

The 1994 election for city council in Rice, Minnesota, ended in a dead heat, so the two politicians decided to settle it with a hand of draw poker. In the first hand, each drew an eight. In the second hand, both were dealt an ace. In the final hand, Mitch Fiedler's eight won over Virgil Nelson's seven.

Not Quite Kosher

As a final act of defiance, a Jewish man condemned to death chose a full-course kosher meal plus a ham sandwich as his last dinner.

Stock in Trade

A carpenter named Palmer was hired in 1634 by the town of Boston to build its first stocks to punish law-breakers. When he submitted his bill for one pound, 13 shillings, the town elders thought the bill exorbitant, so Palmer was arrested for profiteering. He was found guilty, charged one pound, and sentenced to spend a half-hour in his newly-constructed stocks.

~

In the 1750s, a Boston sea captain returned from a three year voyage and was arrested and confined to the stocks for two hours for kissing his wife in public.

Two Dollars an Inch

A woman went into a newspaper office to advertise for her husband, who was missing. When the clerk told her they charged by the inch, she changed her mind, saying, "My husband's over six foot tall, and I don't have that kind of money!"

The quality control department at the M&M company hired a country fellow who threw out all the M&Ms that said "W."

The bicycling fad that swept America in the 1890s put a dent in the hat business, since hats were not often worn by cyclists. One Congressman introduced a bill to require each bike rider to purchase two hats a year.

STUPIDITY

Two morons fished all day in the lake without getting a bite. Along about sundown, they struck a whole school of bass. It was getting so dark they could hardly see, and finally, they had to stop fishing. Before pulling up anchor, one said to the other, "Boy, I sure hate to leave all these fish. Why don't you mark the spot so we can come back and catch the rest tomorrow?" "OK," said the other moron.

As they rowed to the pier, the first moron said, "Say, how did you mark that spot back there?" The other moron answered, "I drew an arrow on the side of the boat pointing straight down to the very spot." "That's good." They walked on up the hill toward town. "Gosh," exclaimed the first moron, "What if we don't get that same boat tomorrow?"

☞ A man called a high-priced lawyer and said, "If I give you $500 will you answer two questions for me?" "Absolutely," answered the lawyer. "What's your second question?"

☞ Making a frantic call to the hospital, a man said, "My wife's in labor and you've got to help!" The nurse said, "Calm down, Sir. Is this her first child?" "No!" answered the man. "This is her husband."

173

SUPERSTITIONS

If you drop a dish cloth...

 omebody hungry will visit you. Someone is coming who is dirtier than you.

And pick it up with your left hand, you will meet a stranger.

And pick it up with your right hand, you will come into money.

And it lands neatly folded, a well-dressed person is coming to visit.

And it lands rumpled, an unkept visitor is coming.

"She was as superstitious as an old granny woman who smoked a pipe and didn't know the war was over."

If you take a bath on Good Friday, you'll turn into a fish. (Texas)

Children who eat mustard have stinky feet. (Texas)

If you sing at the table you'll grow horns. (Virginia)

A knife handle carved out of mistletoe wood has magical powers.

To Have Good Luck...

Rub the belly of a fat man.
Find a homemade nail.
Wear a mustard seed in your clothing.
Carry a black-eyed pea in the left
    pocket.
Receive a letter with the stamp placed
    upside down.
Sleep with your head to the north.

You'll Have Bad Luck if You...

Eat the first snow of the winter.
Find a dollar with a corner torn off.
Look through a key hole.
See a chair rocking without anyone
    in it.
Pull a pig's tail.
Change a horse's name.
Carry a hoe into the house.
Pick up a spoon in the road.

Country Expressions

Busy as a bee in a tar bucket.

Gooder than snuff.

Handy as a knob on an outhouse door.

Mean as a junk yard dog.

So poor, he can't pay attention.

Poor as Job's turkey.

"I was so broke I couldn't buy dust."

Sharp as a mother-in-law's tongue.

Dinner Call: "Come and get it before the grease sets up."

"We were so poor, that when my little brother swallowed a nickel, we followed him around for three days with a stick."

Nervous as a...

Worm in hot ashes.
Tree at a dog show.
Cat in a room full of rocking chairs.

TALKING COUNTRY

Measuring Distances

If you get lost while traveling in the South, particularly in the backwoods, you had best know the lingo. In case you're lucky enough to find someone to give you directions, here are some of the terms you might hear.

"A far piece." This means a gagillion miles. If you hear this term, you might as well forget going there. It's so far, you'll never get there in one lifetime.

"A right smart piece." This is somewhat less than "a far piece." Pack a lunch.

"A little piece" is about the same as "two whoops and a holler."

"No piece at all" would lead you to believe that you're practically already there, but that's not quite true. To accurately gauge "no piece at all," take a chew of tobacco when you start out. After you've walked far enough so that the flavor is gone, you've come "no piece at all." (*Greetings from Old Kentucky* by Allan M. Trout, 1947)

One farmer was widely known as a habitual liar. He had such a reputation for telling lies that his wife had to call his hogs for him.

Another farmer's land was so steep...

His dog had to dig a place to sit down and howl.

He used to plant buckwheat with a breech loader.

He bumped his nose when he walked on it.

He couldn't farm it, but he could sorta lean against it.

World Champion Liar Contest

Burlington, Wisconsin, has the distinction of hosting the World Champion Liar Contest. The president of organization that sponsors the contest says the competition is open to anyone except politicians.

> *"Politicians tell so many lies that we consider them 'professionals.' Right after an election it's hard to find a good lie because they get all used up by the politicians."*

My favorite tall tale was the 1941 winning entry at the Burlington, Wisconsin championship. On his deathbed, the town's best fisherman divulged his secret for catching fish. In a feeble voice, he said, "All I do is sprinkle hair restoring tonic on the water. Then I hold a barber's pole in one hand and a net in the other. When the fish come to the surface I shout *NEXT!*"

One cold winter a curious fellow wanted to see how fast a tea kettle filled with boiling water would freeze. He set it outside, and minutes later he went out to check it. Not only had the kettle of boiling water frozen solid, but the ice was still warm!

Ants

Ants stretch when they wake up in the morning!

There are more than 8,000 different kinds of ants.

Estimated number of ant farms sold each hour: 46.

Butterflies

Butterflies taste with their feet.

Some butterflies are known to migrate up to a thousand miles, just like many birds.

Camels

Camel's milk does not curdle.

Only camels, cats and giraffes walk by moving both legs on one side at the same time.

Cows

A cow's sweat glands are in the nose.

A group of twelve or more cows is called a flink.

Cattle were first branded in ancient Egypt over 4,000 years ago.

India is the only country that has a bill-of-rights for cows.

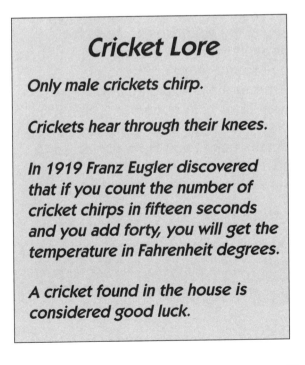

Cricket Lore

Only male crickets chirp.

Crickets hear through their knees.

In 1919 Franz Eugler discovered that if you count the number of cricket chirps in fifteen seconds and you add forty, you will get the temperature in Fahrenheit degrees.

A cricket found in the house is considered good luck.

TRIVIA ABOUT ANIMALS

Crocodiles

A crocodile cannot stick its tongue out.

In 2000 BC, Egyptians used crocodile dung as a contraceptive.

Crocodiles have lived on earth for approximately 200 million years. They have outlived the dinosaurs by some 65 million years.

Dogs

Bosco, a Labrador Retriever, was elected mayor of Sunol, California, in 1983. Running on the "Puplican" party ticket, his campaign manager explained what Bosco stood for: "A bone in every dish, a cat in every tree, and many more fire hydrants." Among his qualifications was the fact that Bosco did not smoke, drink, or chase women, though he did some-times chase cars. He was elected to six terms of office.

Ducks

Baby ducks are born knowing how to swim.

A duck's quack doesn't echo.

Elephants...

are the only animals that can't jump.

only need about two hours of sleep a night.

are the only animals that can be taught to stand on their heads.

"THE McMILLAN PANTS"

$3.00 Per Pair, delivered free in U. S. Send 6c. for samples, tape measure &c. Lawrence, Webster & Co., Malone N.Y.

[1885]

Fleas

A flea can jump 13 inches, or 130 times its own height. If we could do that, we could jump over the Eiffel Tower.

Geese

A group of geese on the ground is called a gaggle. Geese in the air is called a skein.

Grizzly bears

Grizzly bears have been known to run as fast as a horse.

Humming-birds

Hummingbirds can't walk.

A hummingbird weighs less than a penny.

Hummingbirds migrate to South America in the wintertime and return home with warmer weather. They remember where their feeder is and if it's been moved in their absence, they circle around trying to find it.

Polar bears

Most polar bears are left-handed.

Porcupines

All porcupines can float.

Unicorns

A group of unicorns is called a blessing.

WATERMELONS

After he discovered that some local kids had been helping themselves to several of his watermelons, a farmer put up a sign that read, **WARNING! ONE OF THESE WATERMELONS CONTAINS POISON!** When he returned a week later to check on his patch, a note was attached to one of the watermelons that read, **NOW THERE ARE TWO!**

A Florida man picked up a watermelon at a general store in California. "Is this the largest grapefruit you can grow in these parts?"  "Stop!" said the storekeeper. "You're crushing that raisin."

One man's soil was so rich, he had trouble when he grew watermelons. They grew so fast that they quickly  got all beat up by being dragged across the ground. A thief tried to steal a watermelon from that same patch, but before he could break the melon off the vine, it dragged him half a mile.

ne hot Sunday afternoon, a man lay spread-eagle in the middle of a country road. "Old Joe's drunk again," said the sheriff. "I guess I'd better haul him off to jail." "He's not drunk," said one of his friends. "*I just saw his fingers move.*"

"PAPA DON'T DRINK ANY MORE."

Whiskey Superstition

If a girl spills flour while she is baking, her husband will be a drunkard.

WHISKEY TALES

A mountain man came down from the hills and asked for a drink of Old Squirrel whiskey at the local saloon. The bartender said, "I'm sorry Mister, but we don't have squirrel whiskey, but we've got some mighty smooth Old Crow."

The mountain man hesitated for a moment and said, "Look, Mister, I don't want to fly; I just want to hop around a little."

Names for Whiskey

Bottled Courage, Bug Juice, Gut Warmer, Neck Oil, Nose Paint, Wild Mare's Milk, Coffin Varnish, Redeye, Scamper Juice, Joy Juice, Snake Pizen, Tonsil Varnish, Tarantula Juice, Firewater, Tornado Juice, Dynamite.

PURE WHISKEY

WORDS OF WISDOM

"Never hit a man who is chewing tobacco."

"You can estimate a man's age by how far he walked to school and how deep the snow was."

"When you're up to your neck in cow manure, don't open your mouth."

"A day in the country is worth a month in town."

"You can't fall out of bed if you sleep on the floor."

"Never kick a fresh turd on a hot day."
~Harry Truman

"Never speak loudly unless your shanty is on fire."

"If you are corn bread, don't try to be spice cake."   ~Langston Hughes

"When the chips are down, the buffalo is empty."

"A day without sunshine is like ... night."

"Common sense is like boiled vittles; it is good right from the pot, and it is good the next day warmed up."
~Josh Billings

WORDS OF WISDOM

"Even a blind hog finds an acorn once in a while."

"Don't worry about temptation—as you grow older, it starts avoiding you." ~Old Farmer's Almanac

"Don't test the depth of a river with both feet." ~West African saying

"Don't look for dung where the cows haven't been." ~Ethiopian saying

Caution! Driver chewing tobacco. ~Bumper sticker

"Every man has to skin his own skunk."

"If you don't like insects, they will pick on you the most."

"Talk is cheap but it takes money to buy whiskey."

"All you need for happiness is a good gun, a good horse, and a good wife." ~Daniel Boone

"Life is like a roll of toilet paper. It goes quicker when it gets toward the end."

A YOUNG HUSBAND'S COMMANDMENTS

(From the early 19th Century)

Thou shall not have a photograph or any other likeness of any other man but thy husband.

Thou shall not keep the photograph in secret and worship it, for I, thy husband, am a jealous husband.

Thou shall not speak thy husband's name with levity.

Thou shall not find fault when thy husband chews or smokes.

Thou shall not scold.

Thou shall not permit thy husband to wear a bottomless shirt, but shall keep his clothes in good repair.

Thou shall not gad about, neglecting thy husband and family.

Thou shall not strive to live in the style of thy neighbor, unless thy husband is able to support it.

Thou shall not sum up large bills at the stores which thy husband is unable to foot, for verily he knoweth his means.

RECOMMENDED READING

Ault, Philip H., The Home Book of Western Humor, 1967

Boatright, Mody C., From Hell to Breakfast, 1944

Botkin, B.A., A Treasury of American Anecdotes. 1957

Chariton, Wallace O., That Cat Won't Flush, 1991

Chariton, Wallace O., Texas Wit & Wisdom, 1992

Ginns, Patsy, Snowbird Gravy and Dishpan Pie, 1982

Gregory, Leland H. III, Great Government Goofs, 1997

Jayne, Mitch, Home Grown Stories & Home Fried Lies, 2000

Kasson, John F., Rudeness & Civility, 1990

Morris, Scott, The Book of Strange Facts and Useless Information, 1979

Ripley's Believe it or Not, Weird Inventions and Discoveries, 1990

Smith, Richard and Edward Decker, Oops! The Complete Book of Bloopers, 1981

Steele, Phillip W., Ozark Tales & Superstitions, 1983